Kimmie,

To your leadership success!!

Kimmie,

To your leadership
SUCCESS!!

30 Day Leadership Playbook

Your Guide to Becoming the Leader
You Have Always Wanted to Be

Nils Vinje

Get Your FREE Gift!

My mission is to empower you to become the leader you have always wanted to be.

To get the best experience with this book, I've found that readers who download and use the

30 Day Leadership Playbook Quick-Reference Cards

are able to implement faster and take the steps needed to become the leader they have always wanted to be.

Download the Quick-Reference Cards for FREE today by visiting:

30dayleadership.com/quick-reference-cards

To my wife, Annie - Without your love and support, none of this would have been possible.

CONTENTS

Foreword

Early in my career, I traveled a lot. Managing a global team for a company headquartered in the Midwest meant that I was on an airplane almost every week of the year. Given the frequency of trips, I adopted a bit of a routine. Prep for work on my flight out, reading on my flight home.

On one of my trips back home, I found myself seated next to another road warrior. He was at least ten years my senior. He spent the entire flight in front of his computer, while I spent the flight reading my latest book on leadership. About mid-flight, he turned to me and remarked, "I can't help but notice the book you are reading. It is great to see that you are taking it upon yourself to grow your leadership skills. Your company is very lucky to have you."

I consider myself to be a lifelong learner. Leadership requires an investment of time to build skills through training, practice, and feedback. And like any sport, one must adopt a "sharpen the saw" mindset. A leader doesn't simply arrive at the destination of greatness. There is always more to learn. There are always new experiences that require a new set of skills. Leadership is truly a lifelong process.

When I first joined Oracle, my initial charter was to lead a customer success and support organization that came together via acquisition. Five different teams from five different companies. I needed to unite this team under the Oracle banner with one common mission and purpose. This meant retiring the "old way" of doing things, including prior company values and culture.

While my leadership skills and experience to date afforded me this opportunity, I realized that I needed to invest in building my skills in leading this new team. This was a new experience with a new set of challenges. As such, I knew it would benefit me and my team to invest in additional help. That is when I reached out to Nils.

I first met Nils about seven years ago. As an early leader in SaaS Customer Success, I made it a point to connect with fellow leaders in the space in order to share experiences and build a common set of best practices. I led a customer success thought leadership group in the Bay Area and asked Nils to join our small supper club. At these events, I was most impressed with Nils' perspective on not only the state of customer success, but the training and leadership skills required to lead teams in such a nascent space. He constantly challenged us to think differently, lead differently, and to grow as leaders. A few years later, Nils founded Glide Consulting.

I contacted Nils to help me build and lead a workshop with my new Oracle team. We coined this session our Purpose Summit, where we brought together the global leadership team to define the purpose of customer success at Oracle. In preparation for this event, Nils spent time with every leader on the team, inventorying their background, concerns, and desired outcomes for this session.

Nils and I chatted after he wrapped up his one-on-ones with my team. Based on these conversations, Nils recommended that instead of diving headfirst into building our purpose, we should actually take a step back and invest in developing change-management skills. It was a critical "sharpen the saw" moment. A new mission and charter would fall flat if we didn't invest in the change-management skills required to lead this important change.

This initial workshop led to some important collaboration opportunities. With every new post and role at Oracle, a new set of challenges emerged. This meant assessing the current situation, the state of the leadership and management team, identifying gaps, and developing the right training program so that we could come together as a team and successfully lead our organization. Not only is this the key to developing my team but also to developing my leadership skills.

I've had the privilege of working with Nils and embracing the system he shares in 30 Day Leadership Playbook. From Claiming Your Strengths to building The Social Contract to embracing Difficult Conversations, Nils has provided me with the critical skills that have enabled me to recruit, lead, and grow world-class leaders as well as drive significant transformational change. This is a must-read playbook that will truly help you in your lifelong journey of leadership greatness.

As you read this book, may others take notice that you are taking it upon yourself to grow your leadership skills. Your company is very lucky to have you.

- Catherine Blackmore, GVP SaaS Customer Success at Oracle

Introduction

It's hard to become the leader you have always wanted to be when no one has ever taught you or showed you how. As a result, you might feel like you have to figure everything out yourself because you're in this alone. You might feel like you're being set up to fail. You might feel like you are not good enough. You might feel like an impostor who could be outed at any time as a fraud. You might feel frustration from trying to be someone that you are not.

If you have experienced any of these feelings, you are not alone. I have personally experienced all of these feelings at various points throughout my leadership career.

However, I believe nobody should have to feel this way.

I understand the challenges and demands you face as a leader every day. I understand what it feels like to carry the weight of any kind of employee failure on your shoulders. I understand what it feels like when you're at the point of burning out from giving 110% all the time. I understand how badly you want to get to the next level of your career. I understand that it feels daunting when you want to provide the right vision and inspire your team, but you don't know how.

What I have discovered as a result of partnering with hundreds of leaders across all different types of companies is that to become the leader you have always wanted to be, you need a playbook.

This is your leadership playbook.

This is the playbook I have painstakingly built over more than twenty years that I wish I had when I was starting out.

This is the playbook that will not only dramatically impact your life, it will also dramatically impact the lives of those around you.

This playbook is intended for you to consume, experiment with, and adapt to your specific situation.

Remember, the leader that you have always wanted to be is different from everyone else. You are the only one who can answer the question "What kind of leader do you want to be?"

If you don't take action with this playbook, only one thing is certain. The feelings of fear, uncertainty, and frustration I mentioned earlier are going to remain and grow bigger over time. These fears will drive your behavior, and it won't be in a good way. The relationships you have today will not flourish, and you will always have a lingering doubt in your mind, wondering, "What would have happened if I used a different playbook?"

When you decide to take action with this leadership playbook, you will replace those fears with confidence. As a student of leadership, I have personally implemented, tested, and iterated on every strategy and tactic covered in this book. You'll hear my personal stories of success and failure. I'm not going to hide from anything because it is necessary for you to see the good and the bad. Until now, only my private coaching clients had access to these strategies. You'll get to hear stories about them too.

Many of my private coaching clients have been promoted because of our work together. Whether it was a promotion from an individual contributor to manager, a manager to director, a director to VP, or a VP to the C-suite, the reason behind why they were promoted was they increased their leadership skills through the application of the strategies in this book.

I promise that if you implement even just one strategy in this book that it will have a dramatic impact on you and the people around you.

If you implement more than one strategy and use this as a guide for every facet of your leadership, you'll earn the promotions you deserve and will build more trust and respect than ever before.

In addition to reaping the rewards for yourself, you will also positively impact the lives of others. There is no greater responsibility than truly understanding the influence you have as a leader.

If you are ready to replace fear with confidence, here's what we're going to do.

Over the next thirty days, I will give you the tools and coaching to tackle the four pillars of this leadership playbook:

Pillar 1: Leading Yourself
Pillar 2: Leading Others
Pillar 3: Leading with Communication
Pillar 4: Leading with Metrics

I recommend starting with the first Pillar, "Leading Yourself," because everything starts with you. This is where I begin with my private clients as well. In this section, we'll lay the foundation for what you need to be successful as a leader in today's complex world. Then, you can skip to whatever Pillar and chapter is most important given your current situation.

If you are struggling with an area right now, skim the Table of Contents, find the right topic, read the chapter, implement it, and then see immediate results. It's that simple. I won't weigh you down with theory or fluff, just real stories, real strategies, and real results from me and my clients.

Why Thirty Days?

If you read one chapter a day for thirty days, you will know more about leadership than most people ever will. However, knowing about leadership isn't good enough. You need to implement the strategies in order to see results.

Thirty days is also the perfect amount of time to implement and test one strategy. Every thirty days, I want you to select one strategy and then set a goal to implement it by coming up with a plan based on the instructions provided in the chapter.

I'm a firm believer that everything you do from a leadership perspective should be in a state of constant evolution. The topics and guidance covered in these pages will give you many years' worth of evolution opportunities, and I will be here to support you every step of the way.

Don't be the kind of person who says "I should…" or "I'm too busy…" or "My company should send me to training…"

Become the leader everyone else admires. Become the leader that employees line up to work for. Become the leader that inspires. Become the leader that everyone comes to and asks, "How do you do it?"

Become the leader you have always wanted to be.

Pillar 1 - Leading Yourself

DAY 1

How One Concept Can Change Everything

It had been seven years since I graduated from college, and I found myself sitting in a classroom again. This time, I was starting an MBA program. I was sitting in one of my first classes after a long day of work. This program was set up so I could work full-time and go to school at night. Even though I was exhausted from the day, I could feel the excitement and couldn't believe I was back in a classroom.

The class I was sitting in was a Management and Organizational Behavior class. I didn't even know what that meant at the time, but it was one of those classes that got put on my schedule. The professor started by sharing one incredibly powerful concept. Immediately, everything from the previous seven years of my professional career became clear.

I flashed back and saw every point of tension in my career and instantly knew why that tension happened. I looked at the company that I gave everything to, that paid me next to nothing, and realized why I really left (it wasn't the money). I looked at a manager who wouldn't stand up for me, and I understood why that didn't work and why I left that manager.

The clarity I gained from this one concept was like a shot of adrenaline running through my veins. That night, I could barely sleep. I was excited, I was engaged, and I knew how much power this knowledge represented. This was absolutely amazing, and it was something I had never felt in my entire life.

I realized that this is a fairly straightforward concept, so the natural question was, why doesn't everyone know about or understand this? As I reflected on my experiences in the professional world up to that point, I realized that the people in the leadership positions in the companies that I had worked for were in those positions because of who they knew or when they joined the company. They really were not in leadership positions because they had great leadership skills.

They failed, in my opinion, and now I knew one of the big reasons why. Those leaders didn't understand or embrace the psychology behind leadership. They were all great individual contributors and very smart people, however, when promoted into leadership positions, everything fell apart.

Two years later, I graduated with my MBA and a 3.92 GPA which was unheard of for a kid who was a C-average student all through high school and college. The reason I was able to get higher grades and have more fun than I ever had in my entire life was that I was perfectly aligned with what I was studying and what I was doing.

When there is alignment between what you're naturally talented to do and what you are doing, passion is released. This theme is going to be a key part of the strategies and tactics in this book.

After grad school, I committed to bringing great leadership to tech companies where I had worked up to this point. Frankly, they were some of the worst offenders when it came to developing leaders. The reality is, they move fast and have so many priorities that focusing on structured professional development is a challenge and not always at the top of the list. It's the nature of the industry.

Other industries do a tremendous job of developing leaders. The big consulting firms, the big accounting firms, they know that leadership takes time to develop, and they build programs to educate and grow leaders over many years. The companies that I was working for looked at timelines in months, not years.

After a few years of being out of grad school and working in technology companies, I felt the urge to push myself again to learn something new. I didn't want another full MBA, but I needed something, and I wasn't entirely sure what it was until I had a conversation with my father. He shared some of the work that he had been doing with his company as a coach.

My dad was a coach at a company where he had worked for thirty-four years. For the first thirty years, he was the CFO, and for the last four years, he served as a coach to the executives and frontline managers. From his coaching efforts alone, he was able to reduce employee turnover significantly. I had known about this but it wasn't completely relevant until now. You know how sometimes things just perfectly come into view at the right time?

After researching many different options, I signed up for a coach training program. Yes, it's absolutely, 100% necessary to go through a training program to become a coach. I spent 120 hours over five months of learning how to become a coach. This process was truly transformational, and it was something that I knew I had to share with others. I also realized that some of the concepts of coaching were so simple and so incredibly powerful, just like the concepts I learned in my MBA.

One of the final exercises of the coach training program was the "Commit" exercise. The teacher took a roll of masking tape and put a line on the floor in the middle of the room. Everyone was standing to one side and the other side was empty. We were instructed to come up with something that we would commit to doing now that we were graduating from this coach training program and yell it out as we jumped over the line.

I took a minute to think about what I would commit to and then it came to me. I watched as my peers jumped over the line and shouted their commitment. Everyone had a big grin on their faces, and to be honest, I was a bit nervous. When it was my turn, I jumped over the line and yelled out, "I commit to sharing my gift of coaching with the world." Whew! I felt a sense of relief and an immediate rush of excitement. I was committed to sharing my gift of coaching with the world. That commitment to myself back in 2012 is a big part of the reason why I wrote this book.

I brought the coaching and leadership skills I had acquired into the companies I worked for and the teams I worked with. As a result of my unique skill set and strengths, every single team that I ran became the highest performing team in the company. Other people continually asked, "How do you do it? How do you get your team to operate at such a high level? How do you keep them so engaged? Why do they always seem so excited about the work that they're doing?"

There is no one single answer, but there are a series of strategies and tactics that I'm going to share with you in this book. If you take these strategies and tactics and implement them in your own leadership playbook, I guarantee you will become the leader that you've always wanted to be.

DAY 2

The New Rules of Leadership

Many people struggle with leadership. Frankly, the reason why they struggle is that they just don't know what they don't know. They think that leadership is some "big thing" that only exists within a select chosen few people. Or, that you have to be in a position of managing hundreds of people or big departments in order to have real leadership. Or, that you need to go to a fancy MBA program in order to learn leadership skills.

I believe that leadership is within every single person. All you have to do is know the rules in order to play the game. There are five rules that I call The New Rules of Leadership.

Rule One: You are the CEO of your career and so are your employees

Back in grad school on a Saturday morning in that first semester, a few hundred people and I were in an auditorium listening to an outside speaker. This was the first one of these Saturday sessions that I attended. I didn't really know what to expect, but I was excited about the possibility of learning from an outside expert.

The speaker was introduced, we all clapped, he walked on stage, stood right in the middle, staring at us directly in the eye, and asked one simple question. "Are you the CEO of your career?" In an instant, I immediately felt uncomfortable, and that question hit me like a ton of bricks. It hurt because I started to flashback to all of those examples and experiences of my career up to that point and the resounding answer that came out of my mouth and came out of my mind at that point in time was "No, I'm not the CEO of my career." I began to get angry.

I was angry with myself that I wasn't making the key decisions in my life and ultimately I was letting someone else decide what was right for me. You see, in those previous companies, I would always go to my bosses and ask them," You know my skill set, you know my strengths, and you know the organization, where should I go? What should I do?" I always asked for other people to answer that question. Up to that Saturday morning, I never answered it for myself.

In an instant, I flipped the switch and I committed right then and right there to always and forever be the CEO of my career. I committed to doing everything possible to make sure that I was the one who was going to make the strategic decisions about what I do, where I go, the work that I do in order to contribute at the highest level to myself, my family, my companies and my employees. I was going to be in charge!

Here's the lesson in this rule: You are the CEO of your career and so are your employees. When you accept and appreciate this, it gives you a completely different engagement model to work with. You are simply two CEOs coming together to figure out how to partner and get the most amount of value out of each other.

The job of the CEO of any company is to increase the value of that company for its shareholders. This is a fairly standard CEO job description. Your job as the CEO of your career is to increase the value of your most valuable asset for your shareholders, which are your family, your friends, your employees, and your network. Your most valuable asset is *you*!

You and your company are going to work together to get the most amount of value out of each other as possible while you're together. Also, recognize that you're not going to be together forever. And that's okay. It's okay when somebody leaves an organization; it's okay when somebody is going to move on and take a different position even within the same company.

I shared a story earlier about my dad, who worked for one company for thirty-four years. I'm still thoroughly impressed by that accomplishment. I've worked for many, many different companies in my career. My goals after this switching point were to ensure that I was delivering the highest value to my company because that was what was required to do a great job as a leader and to make sure that my work with the company was equally valuable to me.

If you're not the CEO of your career, what that means is that somebody else is in charge of your future. You have to wait to be told what to do. If that's the case, I can guarantee one thing: You will never reach your truest potential and neither will your employees.

Rule Two: Personal growth is the new norm

Back in Rule Number One, I said that you and your employees are the CEOs of your career. I also shared that increasing the value of your greatest asset, which is you, needs to be at the top of the list. Since everyone is the CEO of their career, personal growth has to be at the forefront of everyone's mind. Here's the key, you have to be willing to invest in yourself and not wait for your company or someone else to define for you when, how, and where they're going to "invest in you."

In the old days, it was perfectly normal that you signed up for a company for your entire career. And there were various leadership and development programs over time, but you had to be in specific roles at specific levels of your company to even qualify for those programs. Well, guess what? The world of information and expertise is exploding and is greater now than it ever has been, and it is going to continue to grow.

You have to be the one in control, the one who goes out and finds the learning opportunities to support your growth and development. If you are willing to invest in yourself, then the sky's the limit. You can learn literally any skill on any topic from virtually any expert right now from anywhere in the world. Our access to information has never been greater and will only get better and more comprehensive as time passes.

Since becoming the CEO of my career, I've invested over $150,000 of my personal money in myself. Ultimately, this investment has paid the greatest return of any investment I've ever made. If you're not investing in yourself and you're not willing to invest in yourself, then you have to seriously question whether or not you are a leader. A real leader follows this rule and fully embraces that personal growth is the new norm.

Rule Three: Leadership matters

People want to be inspired, they want to be led, and they want to be part of something bigger than themselves. This is how you are going to get people out of bed in the morning. Here's a secret: Nobody gets out of bed in the morning to check things off a to-do list. People absolutely get out of bed to serve a mission, to serve a vision, to serve someone who has great leadership skills and demonstrates passion.

Companies that value leadership by providing support for their employees and give their employees the opportunity to develop leadership skills will always win. Imagine you have a hundred people in your company and those hundred people are rule followers. They just want to be told what to do, come in at a certain time, be told when they can take lunch and a break, and then just do the work. There is nothing wrong with people who just want to do the work. That's totally fine. It's not what I'm getting at.

Imagine, if in contrast to that company, there is another company with a hundred people who all believed in leadership. They all lead themselves and others and love being part of something bigger. Imagine the results that would come out of that company versus the first company. They would be significantly different.

When leadership doesn't matter, what you get is burnout, marginal results, employee resentment, and ultimately, the worst and biggest cost of all is employee turnover. Employee turnover is responsible for the single greatest cost that is taken out of most businesses. It's not just the cost of the individual hired to replace the person who left, but it's the lost opportunity cost of that individual. It's also time that they were disengaged because oftentimes people stop working before they actually leave a company. When leadership does not matter, turnover is going to be high, guaranteed.

Rule Four: Coaches will win the leadership game

I'm a coach. You read my story earlier about how much time I spent learning how to become a coach. I've also spent over 500 hours working with clients one-on-one.

Coaching is what leads to personal growth. As a coach, you don't have the answers. And so when you don't have the answers, the way you work with employees or other people is that you help them discover the answers. Someone will always be infinitely more engaged in a solution that they come up with themselves than if they were given a solution by someone else.

I've seen the difference between the performance of employees, including myself, who are coached and those who are managed. It's night and day, there's not even a comparison. Imagine going to your boss and asking a question about how to do something that you're stuck on. Imagine they simply replied with something like "All you need to do is ABC and you'll be all set." You said, "Okay, yeah, that makes sense."

Now, imagine if you went to your boss with the same question and they responded with something like "Help me understand what you've considered already?"

And you shared what you had already considered.

Your boss said, "Okay. Well, out of what you've considered, what do you think would be the best approach?"

You said, "The first one I tried."

Your boss said, "Great, what do you need to do in order to put that into action?"

Then, all of a sudden, the tone of your voice changes and the pace of your speech increases because you immediately know what you have to do. You figured the solution out for yourself.

In this example, your boss used coaching skills to guide you along and help you get to that place of understanding and ultimately knowing what to do next.

Rule Five: Emotional Intelligence is the new measure of success

Being smart doesn't mean you're going to be successful. Our world today is more complex than it ever has been before. We have more communication, more connections, and more networks across the entire globe than at any point in history. The people who are in positions where they have to work with many different people from many different disciplines and possibly even many different geographies, have to bring emotional intelligence to the table.

Emotional intelligence is a measure of how effectively you can work with somebody else to get something done. If I boil it down to the simplest thing, those who have a high level of emotional intelligence are able to work effectively with anyone. Those who have a low level of emotional intelligence have to be put in a box and given very specific directions and very limited access to other people.

If you're not emotionally intelligent, you're going to be limiting your future because you're limiting the number of people that you can impact. The way work gets done today is fundamentally different than how it was done in the past. It is a distributed network as opposed to a linear or structural piece where each person does one thing and one thing only. We all have work that is intertwined across departments, across teams, across companies. In order to be truly successful, you must be ready, willing, and able to work successfully with anybody else. The fastest way to do this is by having a high level of emotional Intelligence.

The New Rules of Leadership

1. You are the CEO of your career and so are your employees
2. Personal growth is the new norm
3. Leadership Matters
4. Coaches will win the leadership game
5. Emotional intelligence is the new measure of success

Download your FREE Quick-Reference Cards to take The New Rules of Leadership with you. 30dayleadership.com/quick-reference-cards

DAY 3

Leadership - What Not To Do

On Day Two, I laid out the new rules of leadership, five simple rules that everything else in this book is built on top of. Now we need to cover the other side of that coin.

Just as it is important to know what to do, it's equally important to know what not to do. I've got some quick tips and tricks here to make sure that you stay on the right path.

Tip One: Don't do what you've always done

This might sound counterintuitive given that some things may be working just fine; what I mean here is, just because you've always done something one way, don't expect that that's the only way to do it or that it's perfect.

The goal here is to be open, and as you go through this book, take a fresh look at how you've been operating in each of these different areas and find the ones where there might be a big opportunity to try something different.

I've coached many, many leaders and one of my most important lessons is that it's okay to change things. It's okay to blow things up. It's okay because when you destroy or blow things up, chances are, you end up creating something better. The reason for that is that you have new information and new criteria and new knowledge that you didn't have before when you created whatever it was that you were doing. Be open to accepting that you don't have to do what you've always done. Everything you do from a leadership skill set perspective should be in a state of constant evolution.

13

You should be constantly testing, iterating, adjusting, and experimenting. This is really the only way to ensure that your role never gets boring and never gets stale. You never want to get to the place where you sit there and say, "I just feel like I'm going through the motions and showing up to work every day and attending meetings." That is a cry for help, and there is a very low amount of value being realized by both you and your company.

Tip Two: Don't rely on what you have observed

What I mean by that is that we've all had bosses and known or worked for leaders in our lives. Whether it's personal or professional in our community, etc., we've all had leaders. Some of them probably did a good job while others probably did a poor job.

One of the interesting things about our brain is that we typically focus on the most intense and negative experiences to guide us in future actions. In other words, the worst experiences are the ones we remember the most. Think about some of your experiences with your bosses. Do you remember the incredible elated joy that you had when someone really took you under their wing and did a tremendous job helping to grow and develop your career? Or do you remember the time you got yelled at for messing up some report or messing up with a client or saying the wrong thing in a meeting? Chances are, you probably remember the negative experience in a more visceral way and that can have a significant impact on your future actions.

The reason for this is the result of our fight-or-flight response and the need for our brain to try to protect ourselves. This is leftover from our evolution, and it is a very challenging thing to overcome because we have to force ourselves to focus on the positive.

If you allow this behavior of just naturally gravitating toward the more intense negative experiences to drive your leadership, you're going to repeat the same mistakes that were made before you, and probably to you. Even worse, you may not even know it because you think that it's the right thing to do. Somebody else did it in a leadership position, and you trusted that person at one point in time.

Instead, abide by the five rules I laid out yesterday and question everything you're doing. When you question something, you can ask, "Where did this come from?", "Where did I come up with this strategy?", "What was I doing when this was the right thing to do?" Chances are, even a strategy created six months or a year or three years ago was built in a certain situation given a certain set of contexts. Now you're in a completely different situation in a different context with different information, and you may need to make a completely different decision. That's okay. What you'll find is that your leadership is likely the summation of all your experiences, both good and bad, with other leaders in the past. We naturally model behavior.

There are some exceptions, but for most people, their leadership style will be a summation of all their experiences in the past. You can see this in very notable public figures. Look at people whose second in command takes over for them. You'll notice that they inherit a lot of similar behavior as a result of working closely with the leader over a period of time.

My point here is to always question "Where did this strategy come from?", "Where did this belief come from?", "Where have I seen this before?", "Is this the right thing for me right now given the circumstances in my current situation?"

Once you learn how to do something, it usually gets filed in your brain under the "Don't need to revisit that" folder, until something extreme happens. Our brains have a tremendous ability to create habits as a way to conserve energy. If we went around every day trying to solve every single mundane little problem that we've solved before, we'd be exhausted, and we'd have no energy. Think about tying your shoes. How often do you really need to think about tying your shoes?

Your brain never asks, "Is this the right way to tie shoes?" However, when it comes to leadership, if you're operating under that same approach where you don't objectively look at what you are doing, there is a significant chance that you are running the same plays over and over, and you don't even notice it. The risk is that this behavior can have an adverse effect on your employees and those around you.

Tip Three: Don't focus on yourself

Yes, as I stated yesterday, you are the CEO of your career, but that doesn't mean that you have a license to only focus on yourself.

One of the hardest transitions anyone can ever make in their professional life is to go from an individual contributor to a manager. And the reason why this transition is so difficult is that it involves a fundamental shift of your focus. That fundamental shift takes place when you take the focus off yourself and your performance, and you shift your focus to others and their performance.

Some people struggle with this shift, and that's okay. Not everybody has strengths aligned with being in a position where they are responsible for other people's production and productivity. You can still build leadership skills even if you're not a manager. You don't have to technically be in a management position to take advantage of all the leadership strategies and tactics that I'm going to share with you. If I had to summarize the role of a leader in one sentence, I'd say the role of a leader is to do everything possible to make sure his or her employees are successful. Even if you're not a manager, think about the employees that you work with as your employees. These are the people that you count on to get work done. Those are the people you have to make successful.

Tip Four: Don't use command and control

As antiquated as it is to assume that everyone will work for one company for their entire career, it's the same for assuming that thinking a command-and-control approach will work. It's an antiquated leadership style.

The question is, how are you going to ensure your leadership is ready for a multi-generational audience because that's where we are right now. That is also where we will be in the future. The strategies in this book will be as relevant many years from now as they are today.

The application of these strategies may differ, but the principles will remain the same. And the principles are built on the five rules that I shared yesterday. As long as those rules are relevant, the principles will be too.

The world today moves too fast to not engage others and help them develop. In doing so, you will help them contribute at the highest level to themselves, their companies, and their families. A "command-and-control" environment and associated leadership style don't work anymore.

Leadership - What Not To Do
1. Don't do what you have always done
2. Don't rely on what you have observed
3. Don't focus on yourself
4. Don't use command and control

DAY 4

Claim Your Strengths

I joined a company who wore their Net Promoter Score (NPS), which is a measure of customer sentiment, as a badge of honor. The CEO was adamant they would hit the NPS target every quarter, and I felt it would be a great opportunity to join a customer-focused company as a VP, so I excitedly took the role. It wasn't all smooth sailing.

I joined the company in February, and the NPS results of the previous Q4 came in. They had declined slightly from Q3, but it wasn't a cause for concern. Then, in April, we received our Q1 NPS results. They were the lowest in the company's history; the score had been cut by half! Improving the NPS score became an "all hands on deck" project, with a project team that included me, the co-founders, the head of Sales, and the head of Marketing.

We dove into an analysis project to dig deeper and uncover what was going on. NPS measures promoters, passives, and detractors, using a numerical scale. Apart from the number, it was unclear what separated a passive from a detractor. We had an optional question field that asked the customer to share more to help us understand the explanation for their answer. The small amount of qualitative data collected was cryptic, at best.

I took the lead on the project and scheduled ten interviews with our customers. The co-founder and I would tag team on the interviews— one person captured notes while the other asked questions, and then we would swap roles. Each new meeting had a new document, jam-packed with notes.

The documents were very detailed, so I attempted to pull the themes into a spreadsheet and then start deciphering the responses.

We had finished the process, so the co-founder had to dive back into other priorities. I was left with a mountain of data to sift through, and there was one big problem: I didn't have a clue where to start.

I was stuck.

A few more weeks passed, and it was the end of Q2. The leadership team wanted to see action and results. They would check in on the project and ask how things were going. I deflected their questions, citing customer issues and "needing more time" to dive into the details. I kept myself busy, putting out the typical fires that come with running a customer success team because there was always something going on. I was lying to myself. The truth was I didn't know what to do next.

Around this time, one of my employees gave me the StrengthsFinder book, so I read it on the train as I traveled home. I explored the framework. It said, "Acknowledge the areas where you don't have dominant strengths and focus on what you're naturally talented to do and you'll be successful. When you focus on strengths, your chance of success grows exponentially." It made a lot of sense and gave me a glimmer of hope, so I invested in taking the Strengths assessment.

I got my list of top five strengths, and my dominant strength was Maximizer. The description said, "People with the Maximizer strength see strengths in other people before they see it in themselves." "Aha!" moment number one. The Maximizer strength explained why I loved being a leader and a coach. I would overinvest my time in my team to develop them because that's where I felt the greatest alignment and passion.

I continued reading… "People exceptionally talented in the Maximizer theme focus on strengths as a way to stimulate personal and group excellence. They seek to transform something strong into something superb." One hundred percent me. It continued, "Maximizers love to help others become excited about their potential." Yes, yes, yes! After I had finished reading the description, I realized I was a natural Maximizer. Before learning this description, when people asked me what I was good at, I would tell them I liked being a manager and helping people. Now, I had a crystal-clear description of what I was most talented to do.

What a breakthrough!

A few days later, I had a one-on-one with the employee who gave me the book. She shared her strengths profile with me, and her number one dominant strength was Strategic. We read through the description for the strategic strength together, "People exceptionally talented in the Strategic theme create alternative ways to proceed. Faced with any given scenario they can quickly spot the relevant patterns and issues." She was an expert at this. We kept reading... "People with dominant strategic talents have the ability to sort through the clutter and find the best route." The mountain of customer feedback for the now overdue NPS project came to mind.

We continued reading, "This is not a learned skill. It is a distinct way of thinking, a particular perspective on the world as a whole. This outlook allows them to see patterns where others simply see complexity." I saw complexity in this mountain of data, and Joan could see patterns looking at the same thing. "Mindful of these patterns, they can envision alternative scenarios of asking, 'What if this happened?' This recurring question helps them see, plan, and prepare for future situations. They see a way when others assume there is no way. Armed with a strategy, they strike forward. People with strategic talents bring creative anticipation, imagination, and persistence to the groups and projects they complete. They can quickly weigh alternative paths and determine the one that will work best and most efficiently. They find the best route moving forward."

I was overwhelmed, swamped, and beating myself up. As a VP, I felt like I should have been able to deliver the project. As imposter syndrome set in, the pressure of the project was mounting, and the co-founders wanted to see results. As I talked to my employee, I told her, "I'm struggling. I don't know what to do with all this data." She looked at me with big eyes and said, "This is my favorite kind of project to work on." I blurted out, "What? Are you serious?" We teamed up to deliver the project. She drove the analysis, and I supported her through the analysis, presentation, and delivery. We made a great team and loved working together.

When I told the leadership team what was happening, one of the co-founders didn't understand why the employee was going to run this project instead of me. I was the leader of the team. I took some time to explain it to him using the Strengths theme descriptions, but he didn't quite follow. I was comfortable with that because, in hindsight, my responsibility was to deliver the project in the most efficient way possible. We delivered, my employee had the opportunity to flex her strengths, and we turned around NPS by the next quarter, thanks to the initiatives she helped us put in place.

This project was one of my greatest accomplishments as a leader, and I had a critical breakthrough learning from this experience: aligning people's strengths to their work can yield incredible results. As leaders, we're expected to have all the answers and "figure it out." My ego told me, "You're the leader. You should be able to do this. Why can't you do this?" I realize that I could never deliver the project to the same level without my employee's help. I am OK with that because I am not naturally talented to sift through a mountain of complex customer data.

You don't need to have all the answers, but you do need to have a Strengths framework to guide you to the right person for the job.

How I helped a leadership team overcome conflict using Strengths

It's impossible to predict what will happen in a Strengths workshop... and that's part of the fun!

I ran an offsite leadership workshop with a VP and his three directors. Before we started, the team had completed the StrengthsFinder assessment and reviewed their profiles, so everyone had a good understanding of their most dominant strengths.

Early on the first day of the workshop, I noticed something weird. There was palpable tension between the VP and one of the directors. I pulled the director aside after their exchange, and he told me, "Every time the VP comes into my office, he starts jabbering a mile a minute. I tell him to stop, and I draw a square on my whiteboard, and I tell him to draw a picture in that box because I have absolutely no idea what he's talking about."

We dug in to find out what was going on. They were confused. Their interactions were awkward, and this problem had been festering for years. The VP didn't understand why his director was having so much trouble or what he was doing wrong. When we looked at this issue through a Strengths lens, we began to uncover where each of them was coming from and how they processed the world around them.

I posed a few questions, like:
- What do your strengths mean to you?
- How do they play a part in your day-to-day roles?

20

Sure enough, the VP volunteered to answer first. His number one strength was Strategic. Remember that a dominant Strategic helps a person see patterns through the clutter. He was exceptional at analyzing a situation, identifying the issues, and coming up with solutions. He was a quick thinker and would leave other people in the room behind. When we got to the director, we discovered his number one strength was Futuristic. Someone with a dominant Futuristic strength is captivated and inspired by what is possible in the future. Strategic and Futuristic strengths were in direct conflict.

I said, "Remember the box on the whiteboard and why you can't understand the VP? You have your reason right here! One of you comes up with answers before you even know how you got there while the other is looking to the future, considering all permutations and possibilities. There is a massive clash of strengths!"

Instead of accepting the animosity between them, the strengths framework was the language we used to dig below the surface tension. The reason they couldn't communicate was they had different dominant strengths and viewed the same problems in opposing ways.

Through this reflection, the VP learned that going straight to the solution didn't help his team buy-in. He needed to slow down and thoughtfully communicate with his team. A few weeks after the workshop, I checked in with the team. The exercise shined a light on their differences and provided the language to help them overcome their communication problem.

We all make assumptions about why people behave the way they do and what their intentions are. The learning we shared in the session—which is reinforced every day for me—is that each person will take the best action they can come up with based on their worldview, which is shaped by their strengths.

What are strengths?

The research institute Gallup conducted thousands of interviews over forty years to understand what makes a high-performing team. This statement summarizes their research: "The highest performing teams have individuals in roles that maximize their strengths." Simply put, people excel when they focus on their natural talents.

The challenge is explaining what you are naturally talented to do. For example, if you are asked, "What are you most naturally talented to do?", you might hesitate or say, "I don't know." You might be able to explain the things you like to do or the things you hope to do, or the things that are interesting to you. So, how can you explain what you are most talented to do?

Other assessments like DISC and Myers Briggs categorize people with a label, like "Conscientious" or "ENTJ." These profiles are useful, but Strengths provide a language to describe your talents. There are thirty-four strengths, and the Strengths assessment gives you a personalized list of your most dominant to least dominant strengths.

Strengths give you an easy way to describe what you've always known but haven't been able to communicate in the past. This new language becomes a powerful bonding agent and trust builder between employees and leaders. Strengths bring awareness and recognition to the fact that every single person has unique strengths that present themselves in a different way.

If you know what someone's natural strengths are, you can understand a little bit more about their behavior and worldview. To do this, you must accept that their intent is positive and not malicious. When you accept that, then you can appreciate somebody's natural talents and say, "Well, their most dominant strength is X. I need to change the way I present this information to align better with what they want because they do not think the same way that I do."

Claim your strengths

The next step to claiming your strengths is taking the assessment. It will take twenty minutes and requires your full attention. You can access the assessment at gallup.com/cliftonstrengths.

DAY 5

Master Your Time

As a leader, your time is one of the most valuable assets that you have. How you spend that time is incredibly important. What does it really mean to master your time?

Before we get into that, I want to ask you a question. And it's a simple question with only two possible answers. The question is this: Who is in control of your time?

The only two answers are either you or your environment. When I say, "your environment," I mean your emails, your clients, your bosses, your employees, etc. For where you are right now, I want to ask, who is in control of your time? Is it you or your environment?

There's no wrong answer here. But just know that ultimately, whether you think you're in control or you're not in control, you're actually in control of that decision. When I help my clients tackle this one key psychological element, everything changes.

They often feel almost like a victim where they have to do things a certain way. They feel compelled to attend meetings, always be responsive on email, phone, texts, Slack, etc.

When we address this one question, and they claim control, they realize that everything they do, how they respond to requests for their time and how they respond to other people's needs is completely within their control. This is one of the most important elements of mastering your time as a leader.

Once you decide that ultimately you're in control of your time, the next question is, what are the key areas that you need to focus on in order to ensure that you stay in control?

Email

Email is the most prevalent communication tool we have in the professional world and largely the personal world. Email is a challenge because nobody's ever taught how to use their email. This might sound odd because it seems pretty straightforward. You hit compose, write a message, send a message, reply to a message, etc. But nobody ever teaches you how to use your email through the lens of mastering your time.

That is something that I've had the great pleasure to share with many of my clients and have had tremendous results. By implementing one of the strategies I'm going to share with you, one of my clients immediately saved an hour or two every single day. We put that time into something far more productive than what she was doing. She came up with strategies for engaging her customers so she could upsell them a new product. Within a couple of weeks, she had sold over $25,000 of new revenue to those customers as a result of having time focused on more important tasks than just living in her email like she was doing before.

Email can be a problem because it's an incredible context-switching challenge. There is no reason why one email comes in from a colleague asking if you're free for lunch next Thursday and the very next email is from your boss asking what your strategic hiring plan is for the next six and twelve months. What many people do is try to attack email sequentially and get through them all before something else comes in.

Have you ever noticed how the flood of email never stops? It can feel like a 24/7/365 river. The river analogy is quite powerful because if we look back at early civilizations, rivers delivered everything that the civilization needed for growing crops, living and sustaining life.

However, when the rivers overflowed, crops and dwellings would be destroyed. After the flood, the land would dry out and life would continue. What the civilizations did as they evolved was to put in place valves so that they could open and close those valves to control the amount of water that was flowing through the river. If we think of our email as a river, we can implement an artificial valve and put it on our email so that we can open it and close it at specific times. This helps us control the amount of email that comes in, therefore controlling our focus.

This is really all about how we're going to tame our email as one key element of mastering our time. My favorite tool to use here is called

Inboxpause. It's a free tool for both Outlook and Gmail, and you can get it at inboxpause.com. The way you use Inboxpause is when you are ready to see new messages, you click the unpause button. When you don't want to see any new messages, you click the pause button. It's that simple. All it does is hide new messages from view so that you can stay focused on just what has come in since the last time you unpaused your inbox.

Back to the analogy, Inboxpause is your valve. It is going to control the opening and the closing of the email river so that you can focus on the right things at the right time and still work within your email.

Calendar

The next tool we need to focus on when it comes to mastering your time is your calendar.

The way that most people use their calendars is that it's freely open for anybody inside their organization to see what they have scheduled. This allows for easy collaboration and finding time with each other, which is a good thing and a bad thing at the same time. It's a good thing because you can provide visibility and others can provide visibility to you to make scheduling easy, and it's a bad thing for the exact same reason. If there is an open slot showing on your calendar, I can guarantee you somebody wants to take it.

The question is, how should you really use your calendar?

Your calendar should be the single source of truth for the work that you have to get done.

There is work that you have to do in your role, and in order to get that work done, you have to do a series of things. You have to have meetings, you have to do tasks, you have to have quiet time to do strategic work. That is what the calendar is intended to track and organize.

If you have an open slot from 1–3 PM on Wednesday, but you need to do two hours of preparation before a big meeting on Thursday, that's what should be on your calendar, not an open slot. If it's open, and somebody else sees that, they're likely going to grab it and try to fill it up with their meeting. The result is you get stuck in the never-ending back-to-back-to-back meetings all day and then you get to do the two hours of prep for the Thursday meeting on Wednesday night.

How do you protect what's on your calendar?

This is about consciously deciding where you are going to spend your time by defining what the tasks are that you need to get done and then actually scheduling them on your calendar. Yes, I mean physically scheduling time to check your email, work on a project, prepare performance reviews for members of your team, etc.

The strategy one of my mentors taught me was to start with *No* and work toward *Yes*. What I mean by that is any request for your time gets an automatic *No*.

If a request for your time comes in, start with *No* and work toward *Yes*. For most people, the natural inclination is to succumb to the desire to feel good because you were needed for some other purpose and say *Yes*.

There's one other piece about your calendar that is really important, and that is to budget time for chaos. We have to plan how we're going to use our time so that we can be sure that we're going to get all the activities done that we need for our team and ourselves. There are going to be situations that arise that you cannot plan for, and I like to leave about twenty percent of my calendar specifically for the purpose of moving other things around. I will usually put a placeholder around this twenty percent of the time so that I can maintain complete control over it and not let anyone else grab it without my approval.

For example, if a fire comes up and it is a situation where you have to drop everything to address the fire, the project work you had intended to do still needs to get done. What you can do is slot it into another time slot that was part of the twenty percent chaos allocation and have comfort knowing you can still get everything done that day.

When my clients adopt this approach, it makes handling the chaos really easy because they know they don't have to worry about finding time to do their project work and fighting the fire.

These are usually the exceptions, but exceptions tend to happen every single day.

Slack and Other Communication Tools

Slack and/or other messaging tools are a huge part of our communication culture in today's modern world. These tools have done a tremendous job of evolving our communication.

The challenge that arises comes with the nature of a messaging client where you can send a direct message or tag somebody, and they can see it immediately. Oftentimes, the expectation is that the recipient should respond immediately.

If we go back to our original question of who's in control, you get to decide how and when to engage. Everybody else may choose to be like "Johnny on the spot" and respond immediately, but when you respond immediately, you run the risk of not thinking through your response.

If it's a simple question, you can usually get the right answer right away. However, if it's something more complex from another peer of yours in a leadership position or one of your employees or one of your bosses, it's going to require some thought, and that is perfectly okay. You get to choose how you are going to deliver your response and how much time you're going to allow for processing.

When it comes to managing Slack, one of the most important things is to think of it in the context of your calendar where you have dedicated time specifically for addressing Slack questions/requests and it's not just a constant distraction for you.

If you leave it open on your desktop, and you have the notifications going so that anytime anybody anywhere in the world needs you, they can get your attention, you're going to be distracted and your quality of work is going to suffer. What the people who are asking for your time ultimately want is a better answer. What's far more valuable to do is to set aside specific times on your calendar when you will be checking Slack and responding to messages. This might be once an hour, once every three hours, once or twice a day; it's up to you. You need to have specific time dedicated just to Slack so that you can be responsive to the people who need you while still maintaining control over your time and staying focused on the things you need to get done.

What happens when someone isn't able to get an answer from you right away? They always find another way. You don't have to worry that you're the single point of somebody not moving forward on a project. If someone cannot get an answer to a question they have, they will find another way. If you set the expectation with them that "There are specific times during the day when I'll be available on Slack and the rest of the time I'm heads down on my projects because we have to move these forward," you will maintain control and others will respect you.

Priorities

As a leader, you need to have a clear set of priorities that drives all your activity. Simply reacting to what's happening day in and day out is not going to move you forward. It is not going to get you recognized as the leader that you are. What's far more valuable is having a defined set of priorities that you are working toward, either on your own or in conjunction with your team or some combination of the two.

A simple framework that I like to use is called GRIT and it stands for Goals, Rocks, Tasks. What this does is allow you to break down a big problem or challenge into something that is manageable, able to be communicated to others, and able to be tracked and measured.

When I ask leaders what their priorities are, sometimes I will get a response like "Be there for my team" or "Renew customer contracts." Those are certainly a "priority" but what does it really mean to be there for your team? Here's an example of breaking "Be there for your team" down into the Goals, Rocks, Tasks format.

Goal: Be there for my team

- Rock 1—Meet with each team member one-on-one every week.
    - Task 1—Schedule recurring weekly one-on-one meetings with all team members.
    - Task 2—If a change in time needs to occur, give twenty-four hours notice to the individual.
- Rock 2—Provide three hours a week for ad-hoc issues that come up.
    - Task 1—Identify three one-hour blocks of time to use for ad-hoc issues.
    - Task 2—Set expectations with the team about how to use the ad-hoc issue time.
    - Task 3—Share the time slots for ad-hoc issues with the team.
- Rock 3—Go to bat for my team in the leadership team meeting each week.
    - Task 1—Identify areas to highlight each week by the end of Tuesday to share in the leadership team meeting on Wednesday.
    - Task 2—Add a weekly team meeting agenda item to share what I talked about during the weekly leadership team meeting.

Systems

The last area that we're going to focus on when it comes to mastering your time is that of systems. Systems are how everything is going to run. What you're trying to build in a leadership position is a smooth-running machine. Machines are wonderful manifestations of a series of systems. Think about an automobile, motorcycle, a boat; any of those things have many different systems that have to work together and do the same thing over and over in order to produce the result. Whether that's horsepower, movement, steering, etc.

Why are systems so important in leadership?

As a leader, you should not be a single point of failure for your organization. What would happen if you were going to be gone for four weeks and you had to leave tomorrow? You had no time to sit down with somebody else who is going to take over your job and do all the things that you normally do. How successful do you think that person would be?

Would it be really easy for them because you have clear documentation across the board of how all of your systems work, how you run your meetings, how you run your reports, how you deliver your updates, how you communicate with your team?

Or would it be a situation where you have all that in your head and you know how you do your work, but nobody else could figure that out?

Systems give you freedom.

If you can map out all of the things that you are responsible for, including your goals, rocks, and tasks from a systems perspective, you will be well on your way to being recognized as somebody who has everything running smoothly.

One of my clients made the astute observation when we were going through some systems work together that he realized a systems-based approach to his leadership was going to enable him to escape from the "tyranny of the urgent."

For a long time, he was suffering under the tyranny of the urgent. As a leader inside of a large organization, he was constantly pulled in many different directions. When we designed systems and put them in place to support him, everything changed. He had more freedom, more time, more confidence as a result of knowing exactly how everything was going to work. He put the systems in place with himself first and then with his team.

The five key areas you need to focus on when mastering your time

1.   Email
2.   Calendar
3.   Slack and Other Communication Tools
4.   Priorities
5.   Systems

Download your FREE Quick-Reference Cards to remind yourself of the five key areas you need to focus on when mastering your time. 30dayleadership.com/quick-reference-cards

DAY 6

Bulletproof Your Leadership Psychology

Success and failure in leadership, as with most things in life, are heavily influenced by your psychology. What is psychology? I like to think of it as a fancy word for the mental game. When I say the word game, I mean "game." It is a game and you have to play it to the fullest extent that you can.

There are three key areas that I'm going to walk you through. Think of these areas as the rules of the game. Master the rules and you can play the game at the highest level.

Energy

The first area that we're going to talk about is energy. In a leadership position, you have to bring a level of energy that is appropriate for the task at hand. If you're always tired, out of breath, or never excited about the work that you're doing, it is going to be really hard to instill inspiration in others. The people that work for you are going to naturally reflect exactly what they see.

In the area of energy, there are a couple of key things that are going to really help you thrive from a leadership perspective.

Number one is some form of meditation. My own experience with this is in the area of what's called Transcendental Meditation or TM. When I first learned TM, it was the ultimate escape without escaping.

In a leadership position, there is always going to be a lot of pressure and stress. That pressure and stress can come out in different ways. Some of them are probably constructive, and some of them probably are not so constructive.

Before my experience with TM, some of the ways that I dealt with the pressure and stress were through alcohol and other bad habits. These outlets were not terribly constructive for me, but they allowed me that escape.

They gave me that little bit of breather time when I could just let it all go and not think about anything. There was a numbness I was searching for, and alcohol gave that to me.

When I went through the TM training program, I found that after my meditation sessions, I got that same escape and numbness feeling while recharging my body and mind. It was an incredibly powerful experience, and it allowed me to operate at a much higher level once I began regular meditation.

You do not have to pursue TM, but the key is to give your mind, body, and soul a little bit of an escape. That for me is what meditation means.

The second area within energy is sleep. Contrary to popular opinion, less sleep does not equal more productivity. Sleep is sometimes demonized in the high-pressure world of today where we're always on and always available. If your phone is by your bedside and you have the habit of responding immediately when a new message comes in, your energy is going to be drained because there's no possible way you could show up at the highest level at all hours of the day and night. In order to be a rock star leader, you must get enough sleep.

There's no one rule on how much sleep is appropriate, but the key thing to understand is that sleep is just like meditation in that it allows regeneration. It allows time for your body and mind to recover.

The last area on the energy side is your diet. What you eat is your fuel. If you look at the highest-performing people in the world, what do they eat?

Are the highest of the high performers eating things that are contrary to the energy that they need? No, they're eating things that fuel them.

My family is Plant-Based. We've found through testing and iterations—thanks to my wife—that this is the best, most optimal way for our bodies to run to give us the fuel that we need to do our best work. That's the position I want to put myself in all the time. That's the position you should want to put yourself in all the time as well.

Beliefs

The second key area on how to bulletproof your leadership psychology is beliefs.

A belief is simply something you believe. As straightforward as it sounds, that's it.

Beliefs essentially are like computer programs. Think of your brain as a computer—which it is—and beliefs are the programs.

Like a computer, your brain is trying to conserve energy all the time. Consider the example of something mundane like walking. If you didn't use a program in your brain about how to walk, you would spend a lot of time and energy trying to move every single muscle in your body every time you wanted to take a step. You'd be exhausted. You couldn't do it.

Since we have programs about how to walk and our muscles have memory, all of that works together when we want to take a step, and we don't even think twice about it; we just move.

If our brain is conserving energy, what does that mean for our beliefs? It means that we naturally want to play the same program over and over as a way to conserve energy. This is where the source of a lot of challenges in the personal and professional world come from because beliefs are different for everybody.

I'll give you some examples. Take a second and fill in the blank for the end of these statements.

A penny saved is _____

Better safe than _____

Where there's smoke _____

To demonstrate the power of beliefs, a group of first-graders was asked by their teacher to fill in the blank for the same statements. Here are some of their responses.

A penny saved is... "Not very much."

Better safe than... "Punch a 5th grader."

Where there's smoke... "There's pollution."

What did you think about the difference between their responses and yours?

This is an important reminder that some of the things that you've probably believed your entire life mean nothing to a first grader or someone without your same context, history, experiences, etc.

They don't have the same associations. Over time, you develop these beliefs based on your environment, and that comes from your parents, your teachers, your friends, etc. Many beliefs are formed at an early age, and then they typically stick with you for a long time. But here's the good news, beliefs are a hundred percent programmable.

If you find behavior, especially in your leadership skill set, that is not serving you well, the first question to ask is, what is the belief behind this behavior? If you're used to giving feedback in a way that is not well-received, ask the question, "What is my belief around giving feedback?" Your belief about feedback might be that it needs to be direct, it needs to be abrupt, it needs to be very specific, and it needs to be impactful because that's how you were given feedback and how you respond to feedback.

There's a belief in there that was probably shaped by experiences that you had with a previous manager at some point. Or maybe the experience was with a parent or guardian or friend. The question is, does that belief continue to serve you today?

Here's the truth. At one point in your life, that belief served you for exactly the need that you had at that point in time. However, that does not mean that the belief is going to serve you in exactly the same way today. You have to decide whether or not that belief is as appropriate today as it was back at that time when it was formed.

What you'll find most times when you look at these beliefs through this lens is that the belief does not serve where you are, who you are, and who you want to become today. If you're building your leadership skills, and you have a belief around some element like feedback that is not serving you, it's time to create a new belief.

As I said earlier, beliefs are programmable, and all you need to do is define the new belief. Let's take a minute and look at the feedback example. If I were to ask you what giving feedback means to you, you might say something like, "Giving feedback is a way to show my appreciation and share my knowledge with the other person" or "Giving feedback is a way to help someone else grow" or "Feedback is something that's delivered with incredible thought and care."

Whatever your definition of feedback is, it's totally fine. The key is that you have to define what it means for you right now and then you can load this new program into your brain. After you have defined this, any time there is an opportunity to give feedback, you immediately play what the feedback means before you give it.

Literally. Say either out loud or in your mind, whatever you defined. "Feedback is to be given with care", "Feedback is something to show that I care about the other person", "Feedback is…" You are reinforcing your new belief by stating it to yourself over and over again in the right moment. When you repeat it continuously in the right moment, you will reinforce the belief and change your behavior.

Mindset

The third area to focus on to bulletproof your leadership psychology is your mindset. Mindset in a leadership position is all about not having the answer. I know this probably sounds counterintuitive, but if you go into a leadership position and your mindset is centered around you having the answers, you're doing it wrong.

You don't have to have the answer. You don't even have to figure everything out. But what you do need is the ability to ask the right questions.

We're going to go deep on the coaching mindset on Day 18.

And the last area of bulletproofing your psychology is the area of confidence. Confidence comes from a couple of different areas.

Number one: *Claiming your strengths*. We covered this on Day 4. This is all about accepting that you have strengths and focusing on these strengths will allow you to produce your highest level of output.

Number two: *You are your single most valuable asset*. It's all about you. It's not about anybody else. If you claim your strengths and you recognize that you are your most valuable asset, you're in control.

Number three: Realize you've done this before.

Let's look at an example of a challenge: "I'm uncertain about how to create a vision presentation for the next twenty-four months of my department."

Imagine I was sitting there with you. After you said this to me, I asked you, "When have you faced a challenge like this in the past?"

And you think for a minute or two and come up with an answer that you share. You tell me about when you were getting your first job and you had no idea how you were going to get through the first interview. It seemed so daunting to go from school life to a professional life, and you just didn't know what to do.

And then I said, "Interesting. How did you get through that challenging time?"

And you thought for a moment and went right back to that place, and you said, "You know what? I just showed up every day and in every interview. I prepped and I asked people for help. I figured it out every step along the way."

When you tell yourself about a previous time that you were successful at overcoming a challenge, it can help give you clarity on how to bring that level of confidence into this situation.

Even if it doesn't feel like you've done this exact thing before, you have. Or you've at least done something very close in proximity to this. Ultimately, you can balance your confidence with input from other perspectives, and that's where you can ask for help.

Confidence is all about claiming your strengths, realizing you are your most valuable asset, and recognizing that you've done this before. You got this.

Pillar 2 - Leading Others

DAY 7

The Social Contract

The social contract is the unspoken agreement between an employee and an employer.

Back in my leadership story, which I shared with you on Day 1, this was the concept that I learned on that first night in grad school that changed everything for me. This was the concept that had me flashback seven years and see instantly why I succeeded in some situations, failed in others, and why I left companies and bosses.

It was absolutely mind-blowing once I had the framework and understood that there is an unspoken agreement between an employee and employer. When you join a company or when an employer hires an employee, there is an expectation about what the other party will do. On the employee side, they have certain expectations that you will treat them in a certain way, provide these kinds of opportunities, pay them a salary, etc. On the company side, there's an expectation that you are capable of producing a certain level of output.

The challenge is that this is unspoken in almost every single organization. I brought this to the surface in my own teams and in the companies that I joined only after I learned about the concept in order to ensure that I was aligned with the organization and with my team. When the social contract went from unspoken to spoken, it had a dramatic impact on me, my team, and my company.

The real challenge with the social contract comes when one side does not uphold the agreement. This can be very difficult because the agreement is unspoken. Often, whoever didn't uphold it doesn't even know.

Early in my first job out of college, I got hired as an associate consultant at a big consulting firm. The people that I interviewed with and the culture that existed at the company at the time I joined were fantastic. I thought I was so lucky to be working with this group of people in my first job out of college.

Six months after I joined the company, a new boss was hired for my division. Immediately, he became the person I reported directly to. The hard part was that I didn't get along with him at all. Even harder was the fact that he did not represent anything of what I interviewed with and the culture that I expected at this organization. It threw me into a state of turmoil.

Here I am only six months into my first job out of school, and everything was great up to this point. I get a new boss who seems completely contrary to the company culture that I signed up to work for and I couldn't do anything about it. This is an example of the company violating the social contract with me because I expected that the culture was strong enough to where they would only hire people who were in alignment. At this point, I'm forced to report to an individual who doesn't represent any of those values.

It was a really difficult situation, and I did not end up staying at that company much longer because I felt so betrayed. There was a violation of the social contract in my opinion and that caused me to immediately want to detach myself from the company. I felt they had let me down.

I remember thinking, "How could they do this to me..."

After I learned about the social contract, I understood that they didn't do anything to me.

I interpreted the situation as a violation of my social contract, and it hurt. I also realized that the violation occurred without anyone from the company having any idea what they did. This is the problem with an unspoken agreement.

The importance of bringing the social contract to the surface is that the unspoken becomes spoken. When the unspoken becomes spoken, you're going to see all kinds of different expectations that you probably would have missed. You have an opportunity to bring these expectations to the surface with your team, your peers, your company, your boss, your employees.

I've run social contract workshops many times with my teams as well as with my clients.

In the workshop, both the team and the leader come to the table to have a discussion about the respective expectations each has for the other party. My role in these cases is to be the facilitator to make sure everything is on the table and then drive agreement between the two parties. In the end, we summarize all the expectations and document them. Finally, everybody signs and agrees to the document.

After the workshop, we have a physical, social contract that everyone has agreed to. If at any point one party or another does not hold up their end of the bargain, we can go back to the contract and say, "This is what we all signed up for. Help me understand what's going on."

One of my clients recently had a situation where she was trying to figure out how to move one of her employees, who was a little bit frustrated with her role, into a new role. This employee had been with the company for a long time in one particular role but now wanted to change roles.

Over the course of about four to six weeks, my client was working with the employee and other internal departments to arrange for her to move into a different position in another part of the company. When it got close to almost pulling the trigger to transfer the employee, the employee shared that she was interviewing with another company and had been for the last month.

As you can imagine, my client was extremely upset. This was really hard for her to deal with given the fact that she put so much time, effort, and energy into helping this person and wanted to support them. My client had been afforded similar opportunities from the organization which supported her growth into a leadership position.

When I worked with my client through the situation and we talked about the social contract, what we came to understand was there was a violation, not only on the expectation of the employee but also on her side. As she put it, "I wasn't raised this way. You don't do that sort of thing. You don't keep something like that from somebody who's trying to help you. I just… I feel so betrayed."

What I shared was the fact that she has every right to feel this way. I also told her that she needed to recognize that this was just simply a violation of the social contract. "You expected her to never treat you that way. She may never have known that was an expectation. Maybe she didn't have the same upbringing as you did and the possibility of her feeling the same way about 'betraying somebody' is very low."

The way that you were brought up and your beliefs about how to treat somebody in that situation are completely different than hers, and we can't expect other people to know that. You cannot take the line as a leader that "I would never do it this way" and therefore nobody else should if you've never had the conversation and discussed the real expectation.

The social contract is the underlying cause of most problems between employees and employers. Back in that first night in grad school when I learned what the social contract really was and what it meant, I understood that every frustration point that caused me to leave a company was directly related to a violation of my social contract.

Looking back, it wasn't that the companies necessarily did anything wrong, they just didn't live up to the expectation I had as part of our unspoken agreement. I continuously struggled because it remained unspoken until I learned this concept and brought it to the surface.

DAY 8

Emotional Intelligence

I had a boss once that would regularly fly off the handle when anything went wrong. It didn't seem to matter what the problem was, she would just let loose on whoever it was that was at the center of the situation on our team. This created a very, very toxic environment.

At one point, this came to a head with the team and her because it had been happening for a while. She admitted to us that the reason she behaved this way was that she was worried about how the situation would make her look in the eyes of the rest of the company. She was more worried about her reputation inside the company if there was a problem than about the impact on our team. The impact on the team was tremendous.

People left because of her behavior and she had no idea. Her level of emotional intelligence was extremely low. She was simply operating from a self-preservation point of view, saying, "I have to preserve how I am viewed at any expense." Unfortunately, the expense was us, the team.

This is an example of the exact opposite of what great leadership looks like. Her focus was entirely on herself; it was not on our team. Great leadership is all about putting your focus, energy, and attention on making those around you successful and taking the emphasis and the focus off yourself.

Daniel Goleman coined the term Emotional Intelligence in his breakthrough book *Working with Emotional Intelligence.* I first read this book in 2007, and it was a game-changer for me. It was part of a management course in my MBA program. It gave me the feeling and comfort of knowing that the skills I had were actually extremely valuable. I have shared with you that I was never the smartest student in the class. I struggled in school, maintaining a C or maybe a little bit above a C average.

School was hard. Learning was hard. I didn't enjoy it. But I knew how to connect with people, and I knew how to be friendly and warm and approachable. I was the kind of person who could run with any crowd growing up. I did have a group of friends that were consistent, but I could easily join another group and fit right in and then effortlessly move on to another one. I didn't think much about this at the time but upon reflection, I was able to adapt very quickly and pick up on all the information other people were leaving behind about who they were, what they believed, etc. This gave me the ability to accelerate my relationships depending on whatever situation I was in.

In previous decades, IQ was the greatest determining factor of how successful someone was going to be. The problem is that IQ doesn't change much after our early formative years.

Essentially, what that says is that a large part of society believed that your success was largely determined by something that didn't change with you over time.

When Daniel Goleman stated that emotional intelligence is the new yardstick and the level of your success will come down to how effectively you can work with other people, I carried myself with a different level of confidence. All of a sudden, I went from a defeated mindset, largely because of how I compared myself to others in school, to a winning mindset because I knew without a doubt that I could effectively work with anyone to get things done.

In our world today, things are more interconnected than ever before. Our social and professional networks are connected to people across the world. The focus of work has transformed from just doing one thing to collaborating across different people and even countries, regions, cultures, and ethnicities. To be successful, you must have a high level of emotional intelligence, and I'm going to walk you through exactly what that means.

This is straight from Daniel Goleman himself. This is his framework and material. I am providing you with my interpretation. Emotional Intelligence has made a dramatic impact not only on me but also on the people that I have coached in leadership roles. Every time someone improves in the area of Emotional Intelligence, their value to themselves and their organization increases.

The first pillar of emotional intelligence is *self-awareness*. This is all about being aware of your own emotions. We have emotions about every single thing, every single day. Our lives are composed of emotions, it's not just the highs and the lows, every single thing we do is an emotion. It's how we're wired.

As a leader, your emotions are viewed by many people. As you build your leadership skills, know that your emotions and your awareness of those emotions are going to play a big role in how you are perceived by other people.

This complements the second major pillar, which is *self-regulation*. This is regulating the expression of your emotions. This pillar is all about being in control to the point where you are regulating your emotions so that they are channeled and released through constructive means. If you're aware of your emotions (pillar 1), the next step is to impose self-regulation on these emotions so that they are released at the appropriate time.

Being emotionally intelligent is not about just stuffing everything in and not showing any emotion. It's quite the opposite. Being emotionally intelligent means to share emotion and express emotion in the appropriate way at the appropriate time. As a leader, your emotions are being viewed and interpreted by those around you all the time.

The third major pillar of Emotional Intelligence is *motivation*. When you face challenges, especially as a leader, these challenges will directly attack and strike your motivation. Whether it's from an employee, a boss, a peer, an executive, a customer, etc. there will be challenges that get launched directly at you. Your ability to stay motivated to accomplish your goals and what you set out to do with your organization or with your team is going to determine how successful you are.

The fourth major pillar is *empathy*. This is about understanding the thoughts and feelings of other people. There is a quote I love which says, "You can never truly understand where someone else is coming from." However, people leave clues behind them that can inform your understanding of their situation. These clues can read like an open book if you're aware of them and can see them, observe them, and analyze them.

The clues are things like pace of speech, tone of voice, facial expressions, body language. You can discern a lot about someone else's situation and increase your level of empathy simply by looking at the clues they leave behind.

As a leader, you have to become an expert at understanding someone else's world through the clues that they leave behind. When you're able to do that, you're able to transcend to a different place where you can understand them and they can feel understood. When the other person feels understood, you will build trust.

The last pillar of emotional intelligence is *social skills*. This is taking all the data about a situation into account and then determining the appropriate way to present yourself in this particular situation. As humans, we naturally absorb things from other people or a group of people. For example, if you were to walk into a room where everyone's depressed, there's a good chance you'll feel that way without too much time passing.

If you're aware of this, on the other hand, and instead bring a different energy to the situation, the emotions of other people can actually change. Knowing when it is appropriate to do this is a key part of emotional intelligence. In this example, if you are attending a funeral and everyone in the room is depressed as a result of mourning the loss of the loved one, showing up smiling and bringing a positive attitude may not be the most appropriate thing in this situation.

Knowing how to express your emotions based on all the input that you've gathered from the situation will determine your level of emotional intelligence in that particular environment.

Unlike IQ, EQ is something that can be developed over time. It might feel like some people are naturally gifted this way and others are not. While that may be true, we are all starting from a different point. You have the ability to develop the skill of emotional intelligence over time by focusing your attention in each one of these five pillars and working to improve your skills.

In a leadership position, if you're ever in a situation where you fly off the handle or react in an extreme way to a situation, this can destroy trust incredibly quickly. Trust and relationships are built over years but destroyed in minutes. Emotional intelligence plays a key role in helping you build and maintain trust-based relationships.

DAY 9

Feedback Made Simple

Countless books and articles have been written on the subject of giving feedback. There's a lot of great information out there, and I'm going to share with you my simple three-step system for giving feedback when there is some behavior that you observe which isn't in line with your expectations.

You can use this approach with an employee, a peer, a boss, a friend, a family member, etc. This works equally well for managing down as it does for managing up.

As a leader, being able to give effective feedback is a very important tool to have in your toolbox.

My simple three-step system for giving feedback goes like this:

1. Here's what I observed...
2. Here's the impact that had...
3. Help me understand what's going on...

Here's what I observed—This is where you get to be very specific and fact-based about what you actually observed. This is not a place for interpretation or generalities such as "You always..." This is a place to say something like, "In the meeting on Tuesday, I observed that you were very short, curt, and not very respectful to Jane when she asked her question."

Timing—Feedback needs to come close to when the event actually occurred. The longer you wait, the more difficult it is to remember and recount exactly what happened. As time passes, we forget details.

Here's the impact that had—This is an interpretation as it is based on your observation of the specific behavior. Just like in step 1, the more specific the impact, the better.

Building on our earlier example, here are parts one and two together:

"In the meeting on Tuesday, I observed that you were very short, curt, and not very respectful to Jane when she asked her question. The impact that had is that now Jane is hesitant to come to you to ask questions."

Help me understand what's going on—This is where you get to ask a simple question. The reason behind this step is that often, people are not aware of the behavior that they're exhibiting and the impact that it has. The resounding response is usually "Oh my goodness, I'm so sorry. I didn't even realize that I was doing that. I didn't know that I was having that kind of an impact. I understand and see where you're coming from." That's what happens most of the time, and this question allows the other person to share from their perspective what's going on.

Sometimes, you may have wrongly interpreted what happened. The other person might say something like, "I didn't feel like I was short in that meeting with Jane, and she's actually come to me two times today to ask questions."

This now becomes an opportunity to have the conversation about something that you perceived but didn't actually happen. You never would have known this was the situation unless you shared the feedback.

This feedback system is designed to keep everything objective, and it is highly effective at getting to the root cause of a problem. Most people will not realize that they were behaving a certain way and they also won't be aware of the impact their behavior is having. They usually appreciate this being brought to their attention.

Feedback should always be something that is delivered with care. This framework is designed to be as objective as possible. If you share facts, share the impact, and then ask what's going on, you can eliminate assumptions about why someone acted in a certain way.

Download your FREE Quick-Reference Cards to take my simple three-step feedback system with you. 30dayleadership.com/quick-reference-cards

DAY 10

Meetings That Motivate

Meetings have been the butt of jokes ever since they began. What if there is a way to do things that made them go from being the butt of jokes to being a motivational tool for your employees. Would that be worth experimenting with? I think so.

If we look at the main problems with meetings, there are a couple of core ones that come to mind in virtually any company anywhere in the world. There's either no agenda or too little agenda. This is usually the result of a lack of planning. In these situations, there's no clarity on why the attendees are there, and the same question pops into everyone's mind: "Why am I here?"

Somebody called the meeting because they had a need, and the assumption is that if we all get together and sit in a room or gather virtually over a call, then we will "figure it out."

As a leader building your leadership skills, my question to you is, "How are you going to run your meetings?"

You have two options. You can follow everyone else's lead. There's a good chance that your organization is no different from every other organization, so meetings are probably not great.

Or you can do things differently, so you get results. Rockstar leaders do things differently, and they get results regardless of what everyone else is doing.

What happens when you do things differently and you get results? You build trust. You earn recognition. You get people to line up to want to work with you.

The question is what do you need to do to transform your meetings into something that is motivational and gets real results?

If we look at the problems I shared earlier, they came down to the fact that there's too little or no planning involved in most meetings. If we address that, then we have a far greater chance of building a more successful engagement with the group that is coming together so that we actually solve a problem.

Here are the questions to ask for every single meeting you create or any meeting that you are a part of.

Question One: What is the ultimate outcome for the meeting?

This is where you need to get really specific. Here's an example: "The outcome for this meeting is to define the timeline for our new product rollout, including the major milestones."

If we walk away from this meeting with anything less than a timeline and the milestones for this new product rollout, it would be a failure. That meeting would not have achieved the result that we defined.

Question Two: Why do you want to achieve this outcome?

Behind any activity there has to be a really good "why," especially when you're going to get a group of people together. Meetings are expensive. The cost of a meeting is the sum of everybody's costs and opportunity costs from being in that meeting. To make good use of the investment, there has to be a compelling reason why the meeting is happening.

Building on our example, here's a "why" for that particular meeting: "We must develop a timeline to communicate with our customers and partners so they're aware of when the new product is coming."

Question Three: What is the agenda I need to run?

This is where we sit down before we've even sent the invites and construct the agenda. Here's a sample agenda building on our example.

Agenda item #1—Share the current state of the new product.

Agenda item #2—Discuss and agree to the major milestones we need to define to support our product rollout strategy.

Agenda item #3—Discuss the activities that must be complete in order to meet the milestones from agenda item #2.

Agenda item #4—Discuss the risks associated with the activities and achieving the milestones.

Agenda item #5—Agree and commit to a timeline that we can share with our customers and our partners.

If you understood the outcome and the "why" for that meeting and then saw the five-point agenda above, would you feel good about attending that meeting if you had a part to play in getting to the outcome?

I'd be willing to bet that the answer is probably yes.

Contrast that with a meeting request from one person with six people on the list that simply said in the title "Discuss the timeline for our new product."

Would you attend that meeting? No! You have no idea what the agenda is; you have no idea what value you're going to add or what role you're going to play. It would be a waste of time for you to be in that meeting.

Question Four: Who are the attendees I need to accomplish my agenda?

Based on the agenda—which is ultimately going to get us to our outcome, which will fulfill our "why"—who are the people that I need in the room or on the phone, and what are the roles that they're going to play? When you align the agenda, outcome, and attendees, you can really understand whether the attendees represent all the right people and/or teams (the voices) that need to be there.

Question Five: Is a meeting the most effective way for me to achieve this outcome?

After going through the previous four steps, you might find that you don't actually need a meeting. Maybe getting to the outcome can be done more effectively and efficiently if you used a different approach, like a shared document, a Slack channel, a recorded message, etc. This question should be answered with a yes or no. If the answer is *No*, then you need to explore the alternatives. If the answer is *Yes*, then by all means go ahead with the meeting because it's the most appropriate format.

Recurring Meetings

Everyone has recurring meetings on their calendar, whether they're weekly, monthly, quarterly, or annual. Have you ever noticed how hard it is to cancel a recurring meeting? I don't mean hard physically—you could hit the delete button—but hard psychologically when you think about canceling the meeting.

Have you ever noticed how the meetings don't tend to change very often? Recurring meetings will likely stay the same. They might have been really good at first, but then nobody wants to cancel it, so it just keeps on running in the same way in perpetuity until something big changes.

Why do you think that happens? It has to do with inertia, which means that it's easier to keep doing the same thing than it is to change. As we've talked about before, leadership and your leadership skills are all about constantly evolving what is working and what is not working.

It's completely okay to blow up meetings by deleting them and coming up with entirely new ways to approach getting to the outcome you need. I want to be clear: You have my complete permission to blow up meetings by deleting them.

Use the questions I shared previously to look at every single meeting you have and if you can't answer the questions, especially the outcome one, drop the meeting. Just remove it from your calendar. The trust and respect you will gain as a leader will increase if you handle meetings this way.

Can you walk out on a meeting?

Yes, absolutely. I have. Just because someone else put their meeting on your calendar—without the appropriate preparation, such as described above—does not mean you have to be there. If you don't contribute value to a meeting, you need to leave! Sitting in the room or on the phone is actually worse than you not being there. Even if you're not paying attention and doing something else, you are distracting from the room and you're distracted, too. So whatever you're doing is going to be half as good as if you were sitting and focused on that work.

If you can't answer the question "What value do I add in this meeting?" I hereby grant you permission to *get up and leave*!

Can you decline a meeting?

Yes, absolutely. If there's no agenda, you know the organizer does not respect everyone's time and they probably don't respect their own time. If they didn't take the time to write the agenda for how five people will spend an hour of their time, there's no way that the meeting will be productive.

As humans, we will always use as much time as we're given. But as a leader, you must see and act differently. If you're ever uncertain about whether or not you should be part of a meeting that you got invited to, just reply to the invitation and ask for the agenda. Here's a simple template you can use or modify.

"Hi, thanks for inviting me to this meeting. I'm curious about the agenda. I need to see that before I can decide whether I'm the most appropriate person to attend.

Thanks, [Your name]"

DAY 11

Building A Team Identity

When I graduated from grad school, someone gave me a gift, and it was a Montblanc pen. Up until this point, I had heard of Montblanc pens and assumed they were just several-hundred-dollar fancy pens. I never had a desire to own one, but I received this one as a gift. At this time, I had just graduated from my MBA program with a 3.92 GPA, which for me, was a major accomplishment as I have shared previously. I graduated very happy and satisfied with what I had accomplished, but I didn't know what to make of this pen until I read the little pamphlet that came with it.

The pamphlet described what was at the top of the pen. There was a little white cloud-looking thing suspended in a clear area. What I found out was that this cloud represented the pinnacle, the top of the mountain, the height of your achievement, and that you don't settle for anything less. Montblanc is the second-highest mountain in Europe and the highest peak in the Alps.

I was very much taken aback because I had rarely had that much of an association with a brand. Instantly, it felt as if these people knew who I was. They knew what I accomplished, and this was a symbol that I could use to remind myself of what I overcame. Every time I looked at that little cloud piece at the end of the pen when I was in a meeting, I knew exactly what it stood for.

I went on to use that pen for the next seven years almost exclusively because I loved the feeling I got when I looked at the cloud. That type of identity is so powerful because they made very clear what it represented and who it was for. I was at a point where I perfectly aligned with the brand.

Some of the most powerful brands in the world have spent a tremendous amount of time, effort, energy, money, and resources on building their "brand." I like to think that the word "identity" is a synonym for "brand" as well. When you say their name or when you see their logo, you can instantly feel what the brand means and what it stands for. They primarily do this through advertising, product positioning, and packaging. They want you, the consumer, to be able to see an image or hear their name and know exactly what it means.

Ritz Carlton -> Five Star Service

The Four Seasons -> Luxury Escape

What does identity have to do with leadership?

If you look at a team, a team is just a group of people. Any group of people can come together anywhere in the world for any purpose and you can call them a team. The difference between a team and a high-performing team is that a high-performing team consists of a group of people aligned behind a common goal that are all positioned to execute on their strengths.

What do you feel when someone mentions your team or when you talk about your team?

My guess is not much.

And there's a very simple reason for that. Because the team as a whole has not gone through the exercise of defining what it means to be part of that team.

Just as if Montblanc had tried to make $300 writing instruments with no brand and no vision and nothing behind it that said this represents the best of the best. Do you know how many pens they would sell?

None.

Everybody would say, I can get a pen for fifty cents; why do I need that?

Why does any luxury item exist? Because it stands for something.

Every team I was ever part of before I learned and implemented the strategies I'm going to share with you, functioned exactly like this. We showed up, we worked on projects, we went home, we worked for our boss, and it was our boss' team. I'm on John's team, I'm on Jane's team, etc. That was our identity; our identity was the leader. But that's the absolute wrong identity to have because that leader is not the focal point of the team.

What's possible with a team identity?

What's possible is the creation of an incredibly strong bond among a group of people. This bond transcends both personal and professional aspects of life. When you have a strong team identity, there's this feeling that you are part of something bigger than yourself and you're part of something unique and that your work matters. When a group of people feels this way, amazing things can happen.

As a leader, the value of building a team identity is to be able to clearly articulate what it means to be part of that team so that ultimately, you can hold everyone accountable to that standard.

Imagine being able to say, "This is what it means to be part of this team. This is what we do. This is how we do it. I am going to make sure that we uphold this no matter what."

How do you build an identity for your team?

A team identity is made up of three key components:
1.   A purpose statement
2.   A set of three core values
3.   A team brand

Step 1—A purpose statement is simply nothing more than a fill-in-the-blank exercise done in conjunction with your team. All you have to do is fill in the blank for one question. The purpose of this team is

_____.

That's it.

I'll share a couple of examples with you.

The purpose of this team is to earn lifelong customers.

The purpose of this team is to partner with our customers to make them look like rock stars.

The purpose of this team is to deliver feelings of magical power and joy.

These are real purpose statements from teams I've worked with where I ran this exercise. Through this work, we aligned all the individuals on the team, and we were able to be explicitly clear about why the team exists.

Step 2—A set of three core values.

Why three core values?

There's something in the number three that seems to be true for all human beings. We can remember things that come in three.

What are the three values that you and your team are willing to spend more time, effort, and energy on than any other team in the world? That's the distinction you need to get to. If you pick something generic like "integrity" or "honesty," just know that you need to be willing to stand behind the statement that you and your team are willing to spend more time, effort, and energy on integrity and honesty than any other team in the world. When I pose this question to groups, they usually start to really understand what a "core value" means and we begin to search for what's unique to their team.

Step 3—Define a team brand.

A team brand represents the purpose statement, the core values, and it ties the whole thing together. The brand is the name that you're going to associate with your team, just like we talked about in the identity piece at the beginning of this chapter. Remember my Montblanc example where I clearly understood what their brand represented after reading a few short words?

I have created teams myself and with clients called Team Solid, Team Rafiki, and Agents of Customer Excellence.

The brand is what encapsulates everything. When you and your team look at the purpose statement and core values, you need to think of what embodies those. This might be characters in movies, it might be physical things, fictional things, etc. It could be a combination of words and ideas. It could be a completely made-up word.

It's up to you to help facilitate your team in getting to something that they want to be part of. Remember, this exercise is about relieving the pressure from this being your team and shifting the pressure on everybody saying, "This is the team we're all part of. We agree to uphold these values to fulfill this purpose. If we don't, we have the responsibility to hold each other accountable."

Aligning Five Different Companies

One of my clients was responsible for bringing together five different companies to create one seamless customer experience. Her company liked to acquire companies, combine them, and then sell a new product-and-service offering.

You can imagine how challenging it was for my client to figure out how to align five different companies, five different cultures, and five different ways of doing things. She posed the question to me, "How are we going to all align so that we can move forward together?"

I shared my framework of what an identity actually means—the purpose, the core values, and the brand. That was going to be our cornerstone. I ran a full-day workshop with the entire leadership team of twenty-plus people from around the world to agree on the purpose statement, three core values, and a brand.

We did a ton of brainstorming, testing ideas, experimenting, sharing, and getting agreement. Do you know what the result was at the end of that day? It was a brand that everyone could get behind. No longer were they five different organizations; they were all part of one team. They were all part of something bigger than themselves.

They became one team with a very clear purpose statement, a set of three core values, and a very clear brand. They rolled this out to their entire organization of several hundred people. It served to align everyone. It also helped to keep everyone accountable. This was especially important because this company was going through some dramatic shifts. In order to make these changes and instill these principles, they had to hold everyone accountable to a new identity.

The very first time I became a manager

On Friday, I was an individual contributor, sitting right next to my peers at my desk.

On Monday, I was a manager with three people reporting to me, and I was still sitting at my desk right next to my peers.

This was a challenging situation for me. Going from the individual contributor position to a manager position is one of the hardest transitions that anybody will make in their professional career.

The reason for that is because we are shifting our focus from ourselves and the work we produce to others and the work that they produce.

I knew that I had to act fast in order to not have a situation arise where everyone felt like, "I'm just part of Nils' team." I did not want a generic, bland vanilla team that was just a group of people who happened to report to a manager and that was the managers' team.

I got everybody together in a conference room, and I whiteboarded everything I just walked you through here. We defined our purpose statement, we defined our core values, and we defined our brand. The brand for that first team was "Team Solid."

When we looked at our purpose statement and our core values, the word solid just represented everything perfectly. This brand brought us all close together. And anybody new who joined the team was indoctrinated into what it meant to be part of Team Solid. We took this very seriously and held everyone accountable to this high standard.

That's how I transitioned from an individual contributor to a manager and built the highest performing team in the company within a relatively short period. We created an identity that we all agreed to and held each other accountable.

Where do you use your team identity?

The short answer is, everywhere. This has to be something fun. It has to be something you love. It has to be something the team loves. Ultimately, the team is what's going to make this stick. As the leader, you are going to hold them accountable for making sure that it sticks.

After defining our brand as Team Solid, that became the name of our weekly meeting. We renamed the calendar invitation to the "Team Solid Weekly Meeting."

One-on-ones

When you're working with your employees and helping them through challenges that they're facing, you can ask questions around the core values. For example, if someone asks, "What do I do in this situation?" You can simply ask the question, "Which core value do you think you need to employ in this particular situation?" And then you could follow with, "What would you do with that particular value?"

In the team meeting, you can set aside a few minutes every week and ask things such as, "What's one thing you've done this week that reinforces one of our core values?"

The key is to look at every team activity you do through the lens of the identity that you've created and find a way to integrate it.

What does an identity mean for hiring?

An identity gives you an instant scorecard to measure candidates, and it allows you to clearly articulate what it means to be part of this team. You can give candidates the expectation of what they need to know in advance of joining the company. If you expect excellence, you're going to attract excellence.

The problem is most people in leadership positions do not define what excellence means. You have an opportunity to do that through this process. When you have a clear identity, attracting the right candidates becomes infinitely easier.

When you have a shared identity, you're going to attract people who want to live up to that identity. Nobody wants to be the one to let everyone else down. This breeds excellence because everyone is responsible. If the team's time is being wasted, everyone has the responsibility to speak up. This responsibility doesn't just fall back on the leader to play bad cop and enforce the rules or dictate terms.

What does an identity mean for managing and leading?

It's the shared thing that everyone has agreed to. This gives you, as a leader, a foundation on which to stand.

Let's say one of your employees did not act in an appropriate way with a customer earlier this morning. There are two ways to approach the situation.

If you don't have an identity, you're going to give feedback that could be interpreted as accusatory, saying, "You didn't do this well. You should have done it this different way."

I personally have received feedback just like that. In those situations, what I took away was that I did something wrong, and they're trying to tell me what to do.

On the flip side, if you have an identity, and one of those core values was violated, there is a neutral thing that you both agreed to that you can use as the cornerstone for that conversation. It goes like this: "I noticed that you didn't exhibit/uphold [insert core value] on the call with the customer this morning. I'm curious what happened?"

For the vast majority of teams, there is no clear definition of what excellence means. Therefore, it may feel as if you are trying to hit a moving target. If there is clarity of where the target is, this is the identity, then all you're doing is holding people accountable to that thing which they've already agreed to. That is infinitely easier than trying to hit a moving target. Building a team identity is one of the most important leadership skills that I have learned, implemented, and taught my clients throughout my career.

DAY 12

Expectations, The Secret Sauce Part 1

There's one thing that I've seen cause more problems than almost anything else from a leadership perspective, both personally and professionally. It's setting expectations—today's topic.

What is an expectation?

An expectation is simply something you expect someone to do. That's it. It's that simple. If it's this simple, why is it such a problem in our personal and professional lives? I've come to understand through all my experiences that there are two main things that cause problems when it comes to setting expectations.

Number one is a lack of clarity of the expectation.

Number two is the confidence in setting the expectation.

In many cases, expectations are vague or assumed. Anytime you are assuming anything, you run the risk of being wrong. It's nearly impossible to assume what other people think, should think, or are going to do and be accurate.

Have you ever said or caught yourself thinking one of these?

"I assumed he would do X but he didn't. I guess he doesn't really have what it takes."

"I assumed she would complete the report on time. But I guess she doesn't have what it takes to be successful here."

In both of these cases, there is an assumption that was made, which was not explicitly stated. Therefore, the fault falls on the leader, the one setting the expectation, because they did not make clear what it was they were assuming the other person was going to do.

Setting Expectations

Taking just a few minutes to prepare and ask yourself the question, "Are you clear and confident in what you're asking for?" can save you a tremendous amount of time.

Here are some sample expectations.

Example 1: A clear and confident expectation.

"Please have the report draft complete by the end of Thursday and send it to me so I can review it on Friday."

It is very clear that there is a report draft, it needs to be completed by the end of Thursday, sent to me, the leader, so I can review it on Friday.

Here's that same expectation without the clarity and confidence:

"Please complete the report."

In this example, there's an implicit assumption here representing time. You're going to rely on whatever you think is the time that it will take to do this or the time you think it should be done in. This may not be the same thing the other person thinks. They may think they have a week, and when they don't do it by the end of Thursday—which is what you really wanted—problems occur.

Example 2: A clear and confident expectation.

"I need a response from our product team by the end of Wednesday so that I can communicate with the customer on Thursday as we promised."

Here's that same expectation without the clarity and confidence:

"I need a response from the product team ASAP."

What's wrong with ASAP? It does mean as soon as possible, right? If the other person doesn't understand the context or severity of this situation, there's no way that they're going to know what the impact of not delivering on your request is going to be. On the other hand, if you are clear that you have a deadline to get back to the customer on Thursday and communicate that to the product team as the reason for why you need an answer by the end of Wednesday, you're far more likely to get what you need on time.

Reinforcing expectations

Sometimes it takes time to set and reinforce expectations to the point where everyone is on board and delivering against those expectations. I joined a company as a VP. The team I took over was using a tool to support their activities in a very basic way. This tool had all the data and information available about our customers, but the team was only using it for capturing emails that were being sent to the customer and the responses coming back.

One of the first things I noticed when I started was that we made a huge investment in this tool, and we were using very little of it. Everybody was just doing their own thing in an ad hoc way. I set a clear expectation with confidence about how to use this tool. There were specific fields that needed to be filled out by Wednesday at noon every single week. The reason behind this was that I had a meeting with the leadership team on Thursday morning and used Wednesday afternoon to prepare for the meeting.

Even though this was clear and confident, did the team do the work and respond perfectly? No, absolutely not. It took a little bit of time. I never let up on the reinforcement of my expectations. In every team meeting every single week, I reinforced what I needed, when I needed it by, why I needed it, how it would support the team, how this would support me, and how I would support each team member.

Initially, they pushed back on this by responding that this would take more work and that they "didn't have time." I knew that ultimately this would save them time. After a little uphill learning curve, it saved them a tremendous amount of time. Within just a few weeks, they couldn't imagine going back to the old way ever again.

A huge part of leadership is your ability to set and reinforce expectations clearly and confidently.

Download your FREE Quick-Reference Cards to remind yourself of the importance of setting expectations clearly and confidently. 30dayleadership.com/quick-reference-cards

DAY 13

Accountability, The Secret Sauce Part 2

Think about someone in your personal or professional life who has helped you get more done than you ever thought was possible. Maybe it was a teacher, a parent, a sports coach, a professional coach, etc.

What was it about working with them that enabled you to get so much done? Chances are that it came down to something pretty simple. They held you accountable.

In high school, I struggled with English class, specifically grammar and writing. It was my least favorite subject of all time.

As I got close to the SAT Standardized Test (in preparation for applying to college), I knew I was going to have to do some serious work on my grammar skills in order to get a good grade on the reading and comprehension part of the test.

I partnered with my English teacher. She was someone who I respected tremendously even though I didn't like the subject. I committed to showing up twice a week for an hour before school and so did she. She helped me work through all the challenges that I was having. Showing up to school at 6:30 in the morning twice a week when I was a Junior and Senior in high school was a big commitment.

She held me accountable to our schedule, and I was committed to not letting her down.

As a result of our work together, I got a score I was very happy with on the reading and comprehension part of the SAT Test.

Through this experience, I learned that to make a lot of progress in a short amount of time, it's best to work with someone who is an expert in the area where you struggle and have them hold you accountable.

Why is accountability so hard?

Most commonly, I call it the BBD problem, which stands for the Bigger Better Deal. In other words, there's always a bigger better deal just around the corner. The BBD is something that can distract you from what you already committed to. We usually find very creative ways to justify our BBD addiction. Things like, "I'll start tomorrow" or "I don't have all the information I need," etc.

It's easy to fall victim to the BBD.

Where have you fallen victim to bigger better deals in your life? Where have you started projects and then haven't followed through on them all the way? Chances are if you look at each one of those situations, the bigger better deal was something that you wanted more. You likely did not hold yourself or did not have somebody else hold you accountable to what it was you originally committed to.

This works the same with our colleagues, our team, and others in our company. There's always a bigger better deal for everybody on the horizon.

We resist accountability from our earliest days. Think about the people who were probably most influential in the early part of your life and how much of what they did was to hold you accountable for what they said you were going to do or what you said you were going to do.

It was your parents or the people who raised you. What happened when you were a teenager after so many years of being held accountable? You rebelled. You got to a point where you could not take it anymore. Instead, you wanted to create your own life.

From a leadership skills perspective, if you can hone your strength in holding others accountable and even holding yourself accountable, knowing that there's always a bigger better deal for you and someone else out there, you're going to vastly excel faster and more confidently than most of the rest of the leadership world.

How do you hold someone else accountable?

First, you have to have a clear expectation. This is what we talked about yesterday.

Second, as long as you have a clear expectation and agreement on that expectation with the other party, you simply ensure that it happens.

The uncomfortable part can come from not having clarity in your expectations and confidence in your agreement. But with these two, we can remove the personal side and shift focus to a third-party neutral thing, the agreement supporting the expectation.

In the examples from our previous chapter, we had a couple of expectations that were formulated into agreements with a team member.

The first was, "Please have the report draft complete by the end of Thursday and send it to me so I can review it on Friday."

If I were in this position and I wanted to hold that team member accountable, on Wednesday, and maybe even on Tuesday or Monday before that, I would ask the person, verbally, by email or some form of communication, one question: "Are you still on track for completing the report draft by the end of Thursday?"

If yes, great.

If no, I would respond with, "What do you need to get back on track?"

In the second example, we had an expectation with another team. It was "I need a response from our product team by the end of Wednesday so that I can communicate with the customer on Thursday as we promised."

How do you hold the product team accountable?

At the end of each day prior to Wednesday—you can choose fewer days if you like but persistence in accountability is key—you can ask your product team or your primary contact on the product team, "Are you still on track to get a response by the end of Wednesday so I can get back to the customer on Thursday?"

Do you see how we're only focusing on if we're still on track for what was originally committed to? In this example, it was hearing the response by the end of Wednesday, that's it. You're holding the product team accountable to what they've already agreed to. You're not asking for the answer, you're not asking for anything else, you're just asking for their commitment on what they said they were going to do.

Where would a dose of expectations and accountability serve you well?

My hunch is that there are a few things you could come up with. A great place to start is where a deadline has been missed. Was this a case of someone not performing, or was it a case of an expectation not being clear? Was there enough accountability?

Other situations that can occur might be things that are going to be spaced out a little bit. For example, if one of your team members is working on a month-long project, are you holding them accountable every step of the way? Or are you waiting until the last minute to ask them if it's done? Most times, I find leaders doing the latter, and it's really hard because not everybody is operating that same way. When they get to the end and it's not done perfectly according to how the leader thought it was going to be done, then we have problems. The leader never set the expectation clearly enough and did not have enough checkpoints along the way to make sure the work was getting done in the right way and on time.

In my work with clients, I've found that if I can solve two things, I know I can have a dramatic impact on that leader and the team. The two things are clear expectations and clear accountability. That's it.

If you have expectations without accountability—Not much is going to get done and you will be very frustrated. If you have accountability without expectations—You'll have confusion and frustration.

DAY 14

Delegate With Ease

"I didn't know that is what you wanted..."

This was what I heard from a member of my team. Two weeks before, we had agreed they would take over the generation of a weekly report.

At first, I was shocked by their response. How could they not know what I wanted? We talked about it several times; they told me they understood and didn't come to me with any questions. I just didn't understand how they got to this point.

When they explained their interpretation of my request, I immediately saw where I went wrong. I was vague. What I asked for made perfect sense to me because I had plenty of context. Unfortunately, they did not have the same set of context and so they had a completely different interpretation. Since they felt like they knew what I wanted, they did not come to me to ask questions.

After going through variations of this scenario one too many times, I came up with a simple three-step system for delegating:

1. Define what it is that you are delegating with extreme clarity.
2. Set the expectation and gain agreement with the other person/ team taking over what needs to be done.
3. Hold the other person/team accountable by regularly making sure they are on track.

Do you see how delegation is really just an exercise of expectations and accountability?

A Delegation Example

Let's say that you, as a leader of your team, send out a weekly team summary to your whole department or company. You started this team summary as a way to share the highlights and the lowlights from the past week. The weekly update goes out Fridays at noon.

You're at the point now where continuously writing this update is taking a lot of time. It is also not the best use of your time, and you have members on your team who may be well aligned from a strengths perspective with gathering information, summarizing, writing, and sharing.

The first thing to do if you want to delegate this to a member of your team who has shown interest is to define what needs to be done with extreme clarity.

An example: The weekly team summary needs to be sent out on Fridays at noon. It must feature highlights and lowlights from the previous week.

After someone is identified to delegate this task to, the second step is to set the expectations of what it is they are taking over.

For instance, "This summary needs to be written and published to the company, every Friday by noon. It needs to feature highlights and lowlights because we want the balance of what happened over the last week. If you want to change the structure of the update, that's completely fine, but it must meet these three criteria, sending on Fridays at noon, featuring highlights as well as lowlights from the previous week."

How do you ensure the other person has everything they need to get started?

Here's a sample of that conversation after you have set the expectation and gained agreement from the person who will take over.

"What kind of a schedule do you need to run to gather this information and get this out by Friday at noon?"

They might respond with something like, "I could survey everybody on Wednesday, compile the data on Thursday and have a draft ready by end of day Thursday. Then, I would be ready to send the summary on Friday at noon." (This would be a rock star answer).

Chances are you might have to coach them a little bit. Notice that what we did here was ask the question of what this person needed to do. What kind of a schedule do they need to run to get this out by noon on Friday? We did not say, "Here are the four steps you need to do by these time frames because this is the way I did it." That's the outdated command and control style. Asking the question after you set the expectation is the coaching style.

After their response, you say, "Great! I'd like to be involved in the draft review for the first three weeks and then you can take it over from there. I'd like for you to send me the draft at the end of Thursday for the next three weeks. I'll provide you with feedback first thing Friday so you'll have the time to make any adjustments before the noon send time. How does that sound?"

They say, "Yes, that's totally reasonable."

The other person now has clear expectations on what they need to do. You've asked to stay involved for the first couple of weeks, but then they're going to take over after that.

Most people will stop here. They've made a clear expectation and have heard the commitment from the other person on the schedule they will run. If you stop here, you're going to be disappointed because there's always a bigger better deal that can distract them and ultimately cause them to not deliver what they promised.

To combat the bigger better deal, we're going to use... Accountability.

You already set the expectation that you're going to be involved in the first three weeks, which is great. During the first week on Wednesday, you can ask, "Hey, is everything still on track for your first draft tomorrow at the end of the day?"

During the second week, you can ask the same thing on Wednesday.

During the third week, you could test not sending anything and see if they stick to their schedule.

The key to accountability is a balance between finding out if we are still on track or not and being too much of what could be perceived as a micromanager. All you want to do is know that they're keeping things on track because everybody needs accountability to combat the bigger better deal that's always out there.

Delegation is so much more than just clearing things off your plate. It's all about clearing things off your plate in a strategic way that also sets up the other person for success.

Many leaders are in such a hurry to delegate that they get things off their plate only to have them return because it didn't go as planned. You know by now that this is likely due to a lack of clarity of expectations, accountability, and effectively delegating.

How do you know what to delegate?

First, we can refer back to your strengths from Day 4. Remember the story about when I was a VP? I delegated the analysis of my customer interview project to my employee because her strengths were perfectly aligned with the work and my strengths were aligned with supporting her in doing the work.

Make a list right now of everything you're doing on a weekly basis. This should include your regular reports, meeting preparation, emails, etc. that have to get done every single week.

When you have the list, you'll start to see patterns where some of the items on the list are probably good for you to do and some of them probably are not. You can ask the question, "How well is this task aligned with my strengths?" The tasks that go by quickly and are "fun" or "easy" are probably aligned with your strengths. The ones that take a long time or are not of interest are probably not aligned with your strengths.

Next, you can assess whether or not any of the members on your team or in your company have strengths in these areas. The reason why we want to do this comes back to our strengths-based leadership approach. You'll remember that the highest performing teams have individuals in roles that maximize their strengths.

If we can align the work that needs to get done to strengths, we can get work done faster, more efficiently, and at a higher quality than if we just look at everything based on time.

Go down the list and highlight anything that is not aligned with your strengths.

If you have members on your team who you can delegate to, delegate the task following the three-step system I shared at the beginning of this chapter. If you don't have members on your team who can take over, you may need to keep the task until you do have someone who can take over.

Delegating for the sake of just unloading from your plate isn't necessarily the best solution. The goal is to have work that is aligned with the appropriate strengths and have people set up for success.

Download your FREE Quick-Reference Cards to remind yourself of my simple three-step system to delegate for maximum effectiveness. 30dayleadership.com/quick-reference-cards

DAY 15

Performance Management

In my very first job out of college, I worked for a consulting firm. The first time I had a performance review, I rated myself across a number of areas and then I sent it to my boss. My boss did the virtual equivalent of ripping it up and said, "You've got to be kidding me. You didn't do all this..."

I thought I had provided enough supporting material and that I did a great job, but clearly, that wasn't the case.

I'll never forget what he said next: "Take every score down two notches and then submit it again."

I didn't know what to make of this, but I took every score down two notches and then re-submitted it. Then, that was it, that was the end of the conversation! There was nothing else. I had no idea what I did wrong or what I screwed up; I just got an earful about how I couldn't give myself good marks for my performance.

Years later, while working for a different company, I spent hours and hours on my performance review. I was sure that I had gone above and beyond in every way in my role, and I even used quotes from customers and other people inside the company.

I spent extra time at night and on the weekends in order to complete it and send it to my boss on time. She was supposed to respond with her comments by a specific date, but she missed that date by two weeks. Do you know what the response was after two weeks? "I agree with what Nils said" and that was it!

She essentially had nothing else to say. I was left sitting there wondering, "How can you possibly not have anything to say when I spent so much time writing this up?" I wasn't just looking for a confirmation, I wanted recognition for my dedication and performance and I never got it.

You have probably experienced something along these lines yourself, and you'll probably agree with me that performance review conversations can be some of the most difficult conversations.

I believe that if everyone is truly the CEO of their career, then we need to treat them like a CEO. For my thesis in grad school, I even created The Career Board Performance Management System.

CEOs of companies have a board of directors, and they report to that board on a quarterly basis. During those board meetings, the CEO reports on what happened over the last quarter and what they plan to do over the next quarter and into the future. The board provides valuable guidance and expertise in addition to asking tough questions.

If the CEO of a company has a board, why don't we give the CEOs of their career a career board?

The Career Board Performance Management System

The Process

1. Leaders communicate to their employees the goals of the group/division/organization.

2. Employees select two people in addition to their manager to serve on their Career Board. These people can be peers or other managers, but it is up to the employee to choose these two positions. The two board positions are held for a minimum of one year. If an employee is new to the organization and does not yet know anyone, the two board members can be assigned.

3. Employees present their goals and progress quarterly through a presentation to their Career Board.

4. The Career Board actively listens and provides feedback during the presentations.

How is the Career Board model different?

Employee Mentality

The ultimate goal of any CEO of any organization is to maximize the wealth of the company for its shareholders. Every CEO must report the company's progress to its board of directors once a quarter. This model works in every organization from large to small around the world. Individuals are now acting as the CEO of their career and their goal is to maximize their own wealth through skills and accomplishments. In order to engage and retain today's employees, companies need to encourage employees to be the CEOs of their careers and provide an environment that treats them like a CEO. This will allow employees to fully internalize their goals and hold themselves responsible for their own advancement.

Manager and Employee Relationship

Performance appraisals that only involve a manager and an employee can be difficult as a result of being put in an unfamiliar situation once or twice a year. On a daily basis, managers typically prepare for meetings, attend meetings, contribute, and give feedback during meetings. With the Career Board approach, what the manager is involved in is the exact same thing they do every day. Together with the fact that the Career Board is composed of two other people aside from just the manager relieves some of the strain put on the manager in a one-on-one relationship.

Goals and Personal Exposure

In traditional performance appraisal systems, managers may have gathered feedback from other employees and presented this information anonymously during the appraisal process. With the Career Board approach, the other employees will be directly involved in the process on a quarterly basis and subsequently will be able to offer guidance and feedback throughout the year.

Regardless of the appraisal system used, an employee's goals are typically only known to the manager and the employee. However, by including the two additional career board members in the quarterly presentations, the employee will expose his or her goals to two more people. Gaining perspective and direction from these board members will help the employee establish and achieve their goals.

Skills developed as part of the appraisal system

Performance appraisals typically don't serve as a means for an employee to develop skills, although they are intended to identify what skills need to be developed. Through the career board performance appraisal system, the employee will have the opportunity to develop the following:

1.   Presentation skills—An employee must learn to be confident about his or her accomplishments and present them to the board. He or she must also learn to handle both positive and negative feedback from the board.

2.   Selling skills—The employee must prepare the presentation as if they are "selling" their accomplishments to the board. They must understand how to present their information in a manner that is in line with the needs of the board.

3.   Networking skills—Because the career board is made up of two other people besides the employee's manager, the employee must seek out and find these other people to serve on his or her board. Employees will be encouraged to network within their organization and get to know other employees on a much deeper level by inviting them to participate in their career board.

4.   Competition—By participating in other career boards, employees will see the goals their colleagues are trying to achieve and how they are going about achieving those goals. This visibility will stimulate competition among employees and encourage them to learn and grow by watching others.

The Results

I rolled this system out at two different companies and had tremendous success. The resounding feedback from the managers' side was, "I loved how easy it was for me to get this person's presentation, review it, think about it, prepare for the meeting, show up to the meeting, listen, and give feedback. It just made the performance conversations so much easier. It wasn't me telling them what they did or did not do. I was simply participating in their conversation and that was huge."

As a manager and a leader myself, I noticed that my employees put more effort into this than almost anything else because they had to tell their story. And they had to tell it in a unique way that was up to them.

From the employees' perspective, at first there was a little hesitation because they felt like this was a lot of work. When they realized that this was all about them and it was their chance to tell a story in their own words about their accomplishments and their plans, they realized that this was a huge opportunity. Many times before this, they felt they didn't get to showcase their work because the performance review would happen once every six to twelve months and the specific examples of what they did at each point in time would get lost. Now, they were responsible for keeping track and telling the story on a quarterly basis.

The Career Board Performance Management System is an opportunity to put the ownership of growth and development squarely in the hands of the individuals who are the CEOs of their career.

DAY 16

Guardrails and Freedom

There was a time in my life when I didn't know what I wanted to do. I was fed up with the professional world and always loved working with my hands. I ended up getting a job with a company that built and installed custom cabinetry for kitchens, bathrooms, offices, etc.

One day, my job was to take a stack of wood that would become cabinet doors and drill holes in them for the hinges. There were about five or six steps that I had to follow while working with a machine in order to drill accurate holes. The first set of pieces was interesting because it was new, but then it hit me all of a sudden. My only job was to do a series of steps over and over again. It started to drive me nuts and I was bored out of my mind. Do you know what the machine was called that I used to drill the holes? A *boring* machine! I'm completely serious and not making this up. About a week after this experience, I quit this job.

Sometimes, what leaders ask their employees to do is the equivalent of work with the *boring* machine. There's a big risk here because repetitive work without creativity gets boring very fast. Boredom leads to a lack of engagement. A lack of engagement leads to low productivity.

Even if people say they want to be told what to do, deep down, they have a fundamental human need for variety—for things to change.

We have to orchestrate the work people do from a leadership perspective along the lines of striking a balance.

Too much structure produces boredom, but there can be problems with too little structure as well.

Nobody wants to work in an environment where the rules are

constantly changing and are never clear. Imagine working on a project, doing what you think is your best work, and then coming back only to find out that what you did was wrong.

We all want autonomy and freedom in our work in some form or fashion to feed our need for variety. We each have a different degree of how much autonomy and freedom we want and can handle.

The risk is if you give too much freedom, that can paralyze people. If you give too little freedom, then it becomes boring. So how do you strike a balance between these two?

The solution is something that I call Guardrails and Freedom.

Guardrails and Freedom

Guardrails provide the boundaries to operate within. If you think about driving down a typical highway, what's on the edges of the road? Guardrails. What's in between the lanes painted on the road? Guardrails—just a slightly different implementation. Guardrails define the boundaries of what we can operate within. We can operate our car within this lane, which is within these groups of lanes. Within the guardrails, the individual has freedom to move from lane to lane and to get where they need to go, but they have to operate within those guardrails.

At its core, guardrails are a set of expectations. When you have expectations, what else do you need to bring to the table? That's right, accountability, just as we discussed previously.

I like to use a framework as the guardrails. A framework is nothing more than something that can be applied to more than one situation. Each person and their environment are different in some way.

The framework captures what is universal so that we can use it across multiple people and situations. Using a framework allows the individual to know where the guardrails are while still providing them the freedom to operate within.

One of my most trusted frameworks is something I call PEDAL.

PEDAL stands for Prepare, Engage, Drive, Accountability, and if you do all those correctly, you get Lifelong customers. This framework was created while I was consulting with organizations to help them build long-term strategic relationships with their clients.

As you can imagine, engaging with clients is a rather complex task, depending on the type of environment you're in. Some of my clients had customer engagement strategies where they were very high-touch, and they acted almost as consultants with their customers. Other clients had thousands of customers that they had to engage and educate all along the way through their customer journey. In order to work effectively with my customers and train their teams on how to implement the guardrails and freedom concept, the PEDAL framework was brought to life.

Regardless of the environment or the type of situation, PEDAL still applies. How you prepare for a meeting, how you engage during a meeting, how you drive the actions after the meeting, how you hold accountability for those actions, and how you get lifelong customers is going to change from one company to another. But the fundamentals of what's in this framework don't change.

There is a specific set of steps and a specific set of knowledge that goes along with each one of the sections that provides the guardrails for employees to operate within. This framework gave the leaders of my clients the ability to hold their teams accountable. It also gave the individuals who went through the training to learn how to do this, the ultimate accountability playbook for themselves.

Every employee knew the expectations which came from the framework. As long as they were following the framework, they would be successful because it was designed to address the specific challenges that come with engaging customers and building long term strategic relationships.

Each person had the ability to adapt it to their specific situation. How one person engaged with their client was going to be different than another person. However, the core fundamentals of the Engage part of the PEDAL framework state that there are a couple of key areas to focus on every time you talk with a customer.

In those areas, there are a couple of skills you can focus on to improve your outcomes. As long as the individuals are operating within these guardrails, they will be successful at building long term strategic relationships.

Download your FREE Quick-Reference Cards to remind yourself of the importance of establishing guardrails and encouraging freedom. 30dayleadership.com/quick-reference-cards

DAY 17

What Is Coaching?

One of the first days of my coach training program had a profound impact on me. At this point in my life, I felt like I was in a state of chaos. I can remember feeling an intense pit in my stomach every day that I got up to go to work. We had three kids now: a five-year-old, a three-year-old, and the youngest one was just born a couple of months before I started the program.

I went into the program a bit anxious because I would be leaving my family and a newborn with my wife for many multiple days over the next five months as I went through the training. My wife supported me a hundred percent, and for that, I'm always eternally grateful. She's always had my back.

I went into the first training weekend not knowing what to expect. One of the first exercises was getting an understanding of where you are. We watched the instructor walk through an exercise with one of the students. Then, we were paired up with another student to coach each other through the exercises as a way to experience it and see what it was like to be on both sides.

Do you know what the question was that hit me like a ton of bricks? The question was "What is a metaphor that describes where you are right now?"

Right before being asked this question, I had gone on a ramble of probably several minutes talking about how stressed I was, how I had just started a new job at a new company. I was in a new position that I had not been in before. I just had my third kid, and I was signing up for this program. I felt like I was being pulled in a million different directions.

When the question was asked, "What is a metaphor that describes where you are right now?" I thought for a second and I stopped entirely. This was a very powerful question. I remember the exact spot in the courtyard where I was. The sun was shining, the wind was blowing gently, and I said, "My life right now feels like a Class V rapid."

If you've ever done any whitewater rafting or know anything about rivers, you know they rank them based on class for how turbulent and how many rapids there are. Class I is super calm and very mellow and Class V is intense and crazy—you don't go in these areas unless you're an expert or you're with an expert.

Imagine water crashing over the bow of a boat. It is coming from the left, it is coming from the right, it is coming from the front! That's what my life felt like. I was in a boat going down that Class V rapid, and the only thing I could do was to steer my boat at the last second to avoid the big jagged rocks that were sticking out of the water— which I couldn't see until I was right up against them because the water was so fierce.

I could not see where I was going; I was just reacting and steering away from big disasters that were going to sink my boat. As I shared that vision and that story of where I was to answer that one powerful question, I immediately felt a sense of calm.

I now understood where I was, and I had a starting point to define where my destination was going to be. That simple metaphor gave me instant clarity. I've used that technique with countless others, and it's been one of my best go-to questions to break someone's pattern.

Coaching is a very broad term that has a lot of different interpretations across the world. You have sports coaches, business coaches, leadership coaches, speaking coaches, you name it and attach coaching to the end of it and it seems like it's out there and exists today.

Coaching - A Definition

According to the International Coach Federation, which is the governing body for the coaching industry, coaching is defined as "Partnering with others in a thought-provoking and creative process that inspires them to maximize their personal and professional potential."

Let's diagnose each piece of the definition to get a clear picture of what coaching is all about.

First is the element of Partnering—Coaching is all about partnering with the other person. Coaching cannot happen on its own and it is very difficult or near impossible to coach yourself. There is a partnership that is involved with the other person or group.

Thought-provoking—By using coaching skills, we're going to dig deeper than surface level to come up with new thoughts and ideas just like the metaphor example that I shared above.

Creative—There are many ways to look at or approach a situation. The coaching process is designed to come up with creative solutions to the challenges that are being faced by the individual.

Inspires them—The solutions that come out of a coaching conversation should absolutely inspire action. The key is that the actions are created and committed to by the coachee. Any action that is derived from this starting point is going to have a far greater likelihood of actually happening than if they were simply told what to do.

Personal and professional potential—Everyone has the capacity to grow, and deep down on some level, everyone wants to maximize their personal and professional potential. The challenge is that most times, throughout our personal and professional lives, we don't. We get a lot of opinions about what we should do from our bosses, from our peers, from our friends, even from our family.

What's different about coaching is that its sole focus is on maximizing the personal and professional potential of the coachee, not the coach. This takes the emphasis off the individual doing the coaching and places it on the coachee, ultimately maximizing their personal and professional potential.

How is coaching different?

A mentor has been through the same challenges as you and therefore can guide you through what you need to do.

A consultant is an expert in a particular area and has answers for his or her clients. That's why they get paid for their expertise.

A manager's job is to determine how to most efficiently use the resources at their disposal to accomplish an objective.

A coach doesn't have the answers but has the skills to help the other person discover the answers for themselves. As a result of discovering the answers for themselves, the individual will have a greater level of commitment than if a solution was given to them.

Think about a time when you were told to do something exactly in a certain way or you came to somebody and said, "Here's what I'm dealing with. What do you think I should do?"

And they simply told you exactly what they thought you should do.

How likely was it that you implemented exactly what they told you? My hunch is that it's a pretty low likelihood, and the reason being is that people don't like being told what to do. Even if we specifically ask to be told what to do. Far more impactful is taking the coaching approach and not having the answers, but developing the skills to help the other person discover the answers for themselves.

Do you need specialized training to be a coach?

The short answer is yes and no. I'm going to teach you how to use coaching skills in a business or a personal setting at a high level. I went through a 120-hour five-month-long coach training program and then spent 500-plus hours working one-on-one with my coaching clients. You don't have to go through this level of training to get the essence of what is most important from a coaching perspective. I'm going to boil all this experience down for you into just what is most important.

Why should you use coaching skills?

When you are the only person with the answers, you are always going to be a bottleneck. If you don't use coaching skills with your employees or other people that engage with you, you will not only be a bottleneck, you will also become a single point of failure.

No position in your professional life should be tied to you personally being there to execute it. This is a little controversial because we all think we were hired since we were the best person and ultimately, we're the only ones who can do this job.

The reality is people leave jobs all the time and other people take over. If you think you're the only person who can do your job, then you're always going to build this barrier around you and you're going to be a single point of failure. If something were to happen to you, things would fail. If you got ill and had to step out for a week or two weeks or three weeks, it would fail.

To avoid being a single point of failure, you need to be a leader. From a leadership perspective, the most effective way to grow and develop other people is through coaching. As a leader, you need to be in the business of growing and developing your employees.

What happens when you don't use coaching skills?

If you don't use coaching skills, you can be guaranteed that there will be a lack of engagement with your employees. You will create a team or department with people waiting for instructions on what to do. You will continuously get frustrated that your employees "don't take ownership" and you won't be able to figure out why.

If you've ever said to yourself, "I can't believe I'm so frustrated by the fact that this team, these individuals, these employees, don't take ownership," you're not using coaching skills.

What happens when you use coaching skills?

First of all, you're going to build trust by helping people discover solutions to the problems that they have. You are not simply providing a bunch of directions or facts or pushing a bunch of material on them.

Secondly, your employees will go to bat for you. There is an incredible bond that comes from a relationship based on coaching skills. Seeing the light in somebody's eyes when they discover a solution for themselves and they know exactly what to do next is an amazing experience. As a result, they will go to bat for you because they will want to return the favor since they appreciate what you did.

Thirdly, you can effectively handle any situation. Situations where you have employees who are younger than you, older than you, smarter than you, have more experience in your industry than you, etc. Coaching is the great equalizer, and it allows you to effectively work with anyone, anytime, anywhere.

Remember one of the core tenets of emotional intelligence is your ability to work effectively with anyone, anytime, anywhere? Coaching is one of the single most important skills to be able to do that. You can use coaching skills with your peers, in personal relationships, in any interaction, and have a dramatically different relationship with that individual. When you use the coaching skills I'm going to teach you, people will notice that interactions with you are different from anyone else they interact with. Do you want to have the opportunity to make that kind of an impact on other people?

Back when I was a manager, one of my employees had a Ph.D. and was incredibly skilled in his craft. He was also younger than me by about eight years. For many leaders, this would have been a large threat. Yes, this person was younger, but they had a Ph.D.; that's a big deal. At the time, I couldn't quite imagine what getting a Ph.D. is like but thought that he must be incredibly smart.

One of the calming things for me was just recognizing that no matter what, he was still going to face challenges in our work with customers. The greatest thing that I could do was use my coaching skills to help him work through those challenges because even the smartest person in the world will still face challenges.

I did exactly this and I built a tremendous amount of trust with him to the point where we are still close and good friends today. I love seeing the development that he's taken. He's now a VP in a similar situation as I was back when we worked together.

Coaching is the great equalizer, it will enable you to work effectively with anyone, anytime, anywhere.

DAY 18

The Coaching Mindset

You don't have the answers; that's it!

That's the entire coaching mindset.

This might seem counterintuitive at first. After all, didn't you get into your current position because you did have the answers? Weren't you recognized for having the answers and solving problems?

You might be saying to me, "Nils, what do you mean, you don't have the answers?"

One of the biggest concerns on the minds of leaders I've worked with is having answers to all the questions and challenges they come across or will come across. Sometimes, this can feel like a crippling amount of pressure to always be under, believing that they have to solve or have the answers to solve every single problem that occurs both now and in the future.

If they don't have the answer, they feel that the team won't trust them or won't think they're the leader that they should be. This is one of the reasons that many people who are excellent at the individual contributor role fail when they get promoted into management.

I've seen this scenario a hundred times. The rock star performer who is so good that the company decides to promote them to management because they should be in charge of all the people doing this particular job.

What happens is that the person who was really gifted at his or her craft falls flat on their face because they try to do what they did for themselves with a team. Their focus typically is still on themselves because they were so good at being an individual contributor. They have trouble shifting their focus to their team. They focus on their tactics and getting everyone to work the way that they worked and ultimately people will resist this. Nobody wants to be told directly what to do.

After not too long, the person will typically be back in an individual contributor role either at that same company or, more likely, at another company. This is a huge risk. The reason to promote somebody into management is not that they were great at doing the job. The reason to promote someone into management is that they have the right skill set and strengths to manage and lead other people, not just themselves.

Not having the answers will lift a huge weight off your shoulders. Imagine for a minute, carrying around the expectation that you have to have the answer for everything that you come across. You're not going to know what challenges are going to come up each day, but if you pressure yourself in this way, it would be crippling. You'd never be able to feel comfortable because there would always be something coming around the corner, and it's up to you to have the answer.

Imagine expecting that you're going to face challenges and problems all day long. Imagine now that you are equipped with the tools in your toolbox to find creative solutions to those challenges as they come up. You don't know what they are and you don't know what the solutions are going to be, but you have the tools to apply to those situations.

You really can't ever fail because you don't have the answer. How liberating does that feel? Say it out loud! "I can't fail because I don't have the answer. I have the tools." This mindset puts you in a place of power to be able to handle any situation.

After coaching for so many years, I'm extremely comfortable in any situation with anyone. I even started a podcast called the Customer Strategy Podcast, where I recorded conversations with people when I had absolutely no idea what we were going to talk about until we got on the call. All I said to them prior to the call was to come with the biggest challenge they were facing when it came to their customer strategy and we'd work through it together. It was liberating because I knew that if I followed the steps that I'm going to teach you, I would help the other person get to the answer that they were looking for and we would have a great conversation, which would make for a great podcast.

So much of success comes down to psychology. If you nail your psychology, you can nail almost anything. And this mindset is where coaching begins. Notice how this comes before I teach you the actual coaching process. The mindset has to come first because coaching steps without this mindset isn't going to work. Having the coaching mindset without the steps isn't going to work either. We've established the mindset first and now we can get into the steps.

DAY 19

Five Steps to Coaching Success

Step One—Be present

Being present involves building an awareness of a number of different areas and giving your entire, undivided attention to the other person. This can be challenging given all the things that are normally going on inside of your head at any given point in time. The most important areas to build awareness of in order to keep yourself focused and present are the following:

1. *Body language*—How is the other person positioned from a body-language perspective? What are some of the clues that they are leaving behind? Things like open arms, closed arms, leaning forward, leaning back, legs crossed, not crossed, etc.

2. *Pace of speech*—Are they speaking really fast, or are they speaking really slow? What is their pace of speech, and what does that tell you about how they may be feeling? Are they nervous, excited, depressed, frustrated, etc.?

3. *Pace of breathing*—How fast are they breathing? Is their heart rate high? Are they completely calm? Are they in an agitated or excited state?

4. *Tone of voice*—Emotions carry a tremendous amount of information, especially when they come out in our voice. The tone of someone's voice can provide tons of information about whether someone is excited, not excited, enthusiastic, etc.

5. *The specific words that people use*—Everybody has their own vocabulary. What I mean is that each individual has specific

meanings associated with the words they use. Those meanings are derived from their experiences. It's very important not to generalize or replace their words with your own words because your words are your interpretation. If the other person says, "I'm feeling stuck," you should not reply with something like, "I heard you say you are not moving forward." Instead, you'd want to say something like, "I heard you say you are feeling stuck…"

These are all things to build awareness of in order to help you be present. You may be wondering what to do with all this information.

You are going to do what's called "matching and mirroring."

This is where you are going to reflect back what you have observed in each of the areas above. If you match what the other person is doing and mirror it back to them in your behavior, this sends a signal to the other person's subconscious that says you are a friend and you're not a threat.

If someone is talking really fast, you can meet them by talking really fast. What this does is give their subconscious a chance to say, "They're like me." However, if you were to talk really slowly while the other person is talking really fast, they may get really impatient and think that you are different because you are not able to keep up with them.

Being present is the summation of paying attention to the body language, pace of speech, pace of breathing, tone of voice, the words being used, and matching and mirroring the other person to get into a subconscious connection with them.

Step two—Listen at level two

There are three levels of listening,

Level One Listening is where your focus and attention is on yourself. More than ninety-nine percent of all conversations in the world happen at level one. Everyone is so concerned with themselves and with having the focus and attention on them that they can't wait to say something to the other person. What happens is that one party will be talking and the other person is so excited to say something—or they hear something that triggers a thought in their mind and they want to jump right in. But they completely missed everything else the individual was saying while they were thinking of what they wanted to say. It is not possible to have a coaching conversation at level one.

Level Two Listening is where your focus and attention is entirely on the other person. This is where coaching happens. You shift your focus from yourself to the other person, and they are the only thing that matters in the world right now while you're having that conversation. Earlier, I mentioned that coaching conversations can have a dramatic impact on your relationships and the level of relationships that you have. This is why that happens. When you shift your focus entirely to the other person, things are different. People rarely experience anything like this. You might have at some point in your life come across this if you've ever had a traumatic event happen to you or someone in your family. All of a sudden, all the focus and attention of every conversation you have with other people is entirely a hundred percent on you.

Level Three Listening is where you are so connected that you feel everything the other person feels. You do not have to get to level three in a business context and you should not strive to. This is something that coaches strive for professionally. I have achieved this state myself with some of my clients, and it is an absolutely fascinating experience.

To recap...

Level one—Your focus and attention is on yourself.

Level two—Your focus and attention is on the other person.

Level three—You are so connected that you feel everything the other person is feeling.

When it comes to listening, where you need to be for a business or personal conversation using coaching skills is at level two.

Step Three—Ask powerful questions

What is a powerful question?

Powerful questions break a pattern. We all have "patterns" that we run over and over in our brains. How do you respond ninety-nine percent of the time when someone asks you, "How are you doing today?"

If you're like most people, you say, "Good" or "Fine" or...

What if I were to ask you as a follow-up question, "What makes today a good day?"

I'm guessing you'd have to think for a second and then come up with something to say.

That time you were thinking is when your brain was searching for a new thought because it did not have a pattern ready like it did for the first question.

A powerful question is open-ended.

Closed-ended questions can be answered with a "Yes" or "No." In a coaching conversation, closed-ended questions will leave you stuck with nowhere to go. Closed-ended questions typically start with phrases such as

"Do you..."

"Can you..."

"Don't you..."

"Should you..."

...

Closed-ended questions do not demonstrate curiosity and usually come off as "leading" the other person. Imagine the question "Don't you think we should move the launch date to November?" It's clear that your answer to this question is in the question itself. If the other person simply responds "No," you'll now be on the defensive to try to figure out where to take the conversation.

Open-ended questions demonstrate curiosity. They also have a specific structure that is very easy to learn and implement in every conversation you have going forward.

Open-ended questions begin with "What" or "How."

There is a simple trick to transform any closed-ended question into an open-ended question. All you need to do is replace the beginning of the question with "What" or "How." Here are some examples:

Closed-ended— "Do you think there will be any problems with this project?"

Open-ended— "What problems might arise with this project?"

Closed-ended— "Don't you think we should be discussing this with Jane?"

Open-ended— "What do you think we should be discussing with Jane?"

Imagine being on the receiving end of the closed-ended questions above, and then imagine being on the receiving end of the open-ended questions and note the difference in how you feel. I guess that you'll feel a lot more comfortable opening up and sharing if you are asked an open-ended question as opposed to a closed-ended question.

Here are some powerful questions that are my "go-to's" that you can always have in your back pocket.

What is the impact of... [insert one of the specific words the other person said]?

Impact is a big and important word that will cause the other person to think about the changes that will happen. At this point in a conversation, this is likely hypothetical. This will make the other person visualize the future so that you can help them think through all the possible ways to approach the situation.

Tell me more about... [insert their specific word] or Tell me more...

This is the ultimate get-out-of-jail-free card. If you are ever in a situation where you don't know what question to ask, just ask this question. This works in any situation because the number one topic everyone wants to talk about is themselves. If you ask someone to talk more about themselves, they're going to indulge.

If you could do... [insert their word(s)], what would be different?

This is another future-painting question to get to the heart of an issue. If nothing is going to be different in the future then the action being considered probably isn't appropriate.

What would be the most important thing for you to have clarity on right now?

This is a great one to use when people have a long-running stream of "stuff" going on. They will come to you and say, "I got this and this and this and this and this..." You can break their pattern and say, "Hold on a second, what would be the most important thing for you to have clarity on right now?"

If you could wave a magic wand right now, what would be most helpful?

This question gets the other person to paint a hypothetical future where you're essentially giving them complete control to design whatever they want. But you've given them the boundaries, which is what would be most helpful.

What options have you already considered?

There are things that the other person has already considered and the last thing you want to do is share ideas and have them respond with, "Yeah, I already looked at all those." If you simply ask this question, it will force the individual to recount the options they've considered. If they haven't thought about any options yet, then you can help them brainstorm some options.

How can I best support you?

This elegantly puts the focus squarely on the other person and forces them to get clear about their "ask" of you. In a leadership position, people will often come to you expecting the answer. If you flip it back on them and help them work through the problem and say, "How can I best support you?", they're going to have to think (breaking a pattern) about how you can best support them. They are going to have to come up with something specific right there. If they can't, they can say, "I'll get back to you" and that's fine. The key is, it's up to them to tell you because no matter what you choose, it's probably wrong. That's why we're so focused on getting the individual to come up with the solution, not just you.

Silence

This is one of my all-time favorites. All you need to do is be quiet. As I said before, most people's propensity is to talk about themselves. If you give them the platform and you remain quiet, they will probably continue talking. When they continue talking, they will probably continue to work on the problem in their mind as they talk about it, which will lead to them coming up with a solution. Silence is a very powerful strategy to use as one of your powerful questions.

Step Four—Make Strategic Recommendations

Only after you understand the other person's world by being present, listening at level two, and asking powerful questions can you make strategic recommendations. A strategic recommendation is based on your understanding and expertise. It leads the other person closer to where they want to go.

Sometimes people cannot make the leap from one stage to another, and they need a recommendation. Think of this as a seed you are planting that they will then take and grow way beyond the size of the original seed.

Here's an example of a strategic recommendation. Notice that you don't necessarily need to use the word "recommendation" but that it can be worked into the question to lead them closer to where they want to go.

Based on everything you've told me, what you've already tried, what do you think about looking at this from the recipient's point of view?

Or…

Based on everything you've told me about what you are trying to do and what you have already tried, I'd recommend you look at this from the recipient's point of view. What do you think is most important to them?

Step Five—Set SMART goals.

SMART is an acronym that stands for Specific, Measurable, Achievable, Realistic, and Time-bound.

There's a difference between generic goals and smart goals, and the difference is in the level of specificity. We're going to use this SMART goal framework as a way to engage with our coachees to help them articulate the plan they are going to put into action based on our coaching conversation. As a result, you can ultimately hold them accountable to executing that plan.

Back to the weekly team summary email example from Day 14, here are examples of a generic and SMART goal:

Generic goal: Send out the weekly team summary every Friday.

SMART goal: Send out the weekly team summary every Friday at noon by collecting all the information on Wednesday and having a draft ready by the end of Thursday.

Those are the five steps to coaching success.

1.   Be present
2.   Listen at level two
3.   Ask powerful questions
4.   Make strategic recommendations
5.   Set SMART goals

If you go into your coaching conversations with the mindset that you don't have the answers and then you follow these five steps, you will have a more effective conversation than you've ever had in the past. You will also walk away with specific goals that you can hold the individual accountable to. Best of all, the individual will be driven to accomplish the goal because they were the one who came up with the solution.

Download your FREE Quick-Reference Cards to take The Five Steps to Coaching Success with you. 30dayleadership.com/quick-reference-cards

Pillar 3 - Leading with Communication

DAY 20

The Power of Frameworks

In the early days of my consulting practice, I had an opportunity to pitch to someone who was hosting a conference that I wanted to speak at. I wanted to speak as a way to share my expertise and grow my personal brand.

The organizer asked me what I could present. Essentially, I verbally vomited all over him with all the great things that I did, processes that I ran, and all the little tactical things I did. I didn't have a way to communicate my value. As you might imagine, we left the conversation in an awkward place but agreed to revisit a week or two later.

I knew something had to change but I didn't know what to do.

I called one of my mentors who was a great marketer, and he spent a half-day with me to figure this out.

During this half-day session, I told him all about the things I loved to do. I had a long list of topics (my verbal vomit)—things I loved to teach, accomplishments I'd had, processes I had built for my companies, what I wanted to help people with through my consulting practice, etc. By the end of the half-day, we came up with a framework called the 4 Ps, which stands for People, Purpose, Process, and Platform.

Now I knew immediately how to communicate my value. The 4 Ps framework took me from literally vomiting words all over the conference organizer to a few weeks later having a clear and cohesive message that was easy to understand. I was awarded the speaking gig and had a very successful presentation as a result.

I went on to use the 4 Ps framework for several years in my

consulting business to help people take what was a complex situation and break it down into meaningful chunks. When I laid the 4 Ps framework on top of client situations, we were able to immediately see where the challenges and opportunities really were.

One of my early clients came to me and said, "I have a retention problem. Customers are canceling and I don't know why." A problem with retention is a big problem with a lot of contributing factors.

After I walked my client through the 4 Ps framework, there was a moment of instant clarity. I'll never forget the look in his eyes as he said, "What I see now is that I have problems in the People and Process areas. We can solve those!"

Part of the discussion leading up to this clarity had been around the potential purchase of a software tool designed to help improve retention through tracking and analytics. This solution was created to address the high-level retention problem. However, after digging in with the framework and looking at the underlying problems, it became clear that my client didn't need a piece of software. They needed to solve the people and process problems we identified first.

The most effective way for information to be communicated is to chunk it into groups of similar topics. In my example above, I chunked all of my experience into four main areas: People, Purpose, Process, and Platform and called it the 4 Ps framework.

What is a framework?

A framework is simply
1. The high-level chunks or groups that can be applied and conceptually understood by anyone even if they are not familiar with the specifics of the situation
2. An effective communication vehicle for both internal and external communication
3. Something that can turn complexity, or sometimes even chaos, into simplicity and understanding

Why do leaders need frameworks?

As a leader, you have to tell a story about your work; simply doing the work is not enough.

You have to communicate what can be complex topics with a lot of specific context in a simple way; the simpler, the better.

One of the biggest challenges you'll face is overcoming other people not having context. This applies both internally and externally. Internally, the other departments that you work with may or may not have much context about your work. Even if you think they have context, they probably don't. Externally, the challenge of context is even harder because they are not going to have any context about your environment or your situation, but they need to learn from you.

Frameworks are the ultimate communication tool to overcome other people not having context.

I shared the 4 Ps example already. Another framework I have used is PEDAL, which I talked about on Day 16—Guardrails and Freedom. PEDAL stands for Prepare, Engage, Drive, Accountability, and Lifelong customers. That framework applies equally to one individual in one company as it does to one individual in another company. It also applies equally from one company to another company. It's simply a framework and then we customize it for the specific situation.

The 4 Ps framework starts with the ability to be applied to any situation (just like PEDAL), and then it's customized to a specific situation (the work I would do with my clients).

The customer strategy method was my next evolution from the 4 Ps. The Customer Strategy Method supported the premise that anytime you are engaging with a customer, you need a strategy and it has to have five things.

1. You have to be *prescriptive*. You need to design the experience your customer will go through to get the most value out of your product or service. Your customer is counting on you to guide them.

2. You have to define a *transformation* that your customer is going to go through with your product or solution.

3. You have to have a *fresh start*. At the beginning of your customer engagement, you must capture their optimism and excitement. This is where you are going to set expectations for how you will engage both now and in the future.

4. You must have an *engaging middle*. This is a defined set of strategies to guarantee you can continuously provide value to your customer over time.

5. You have to *crush the milestones*. First, you must define the milestones that your customers need to go through to get value out of your product or service. Then, you're going to track their progress and ensure they crush those milestones.

The Customer Strategy Method framework applies equally to a software company selling a $100,000 a year product as it does to an HVAC and plumbing business selling a service to consumers. I can say that with complete confidence because I've applied it to both of those situations and many, many more.

Why are frameworks powerful?

Frameworks enable you, as the leader, to frame the conversation. In other words, you are providing the baseline for what you're going to communicate to others so that you can focus their attention on the most important things. This is really important because people have a hard time trying to understand something that's completely open-ended.

If you're operating at a tactical level or communicating at a tactical level, nobody's going to have any context and they're going to be completely lost when you start talking about your processes or situations. However, if you provide a framework and you give them the structure for how to think about the problem you are solving, then you're going to have a much easier time getting feedback. They will understand the framework and understand where to focus their attention.

Frameworks are memorable. People can remember a framework a lot easier than they can remember a bunch of tasks or processes.

What happens when leaders don't use frameworks?

They will talk about their accomplishments and work as a list of tasks.

They will struggle with painting a vision that their team and other leaders can grasp and get behind.

If you can't overcome the complexity of the world you operate in through a framework, you will struggle with your communication. You'll struggle, going from one job to the next and doing more than simply executing the same plays from the last company.

Knowing what to do in one role and applying that to another role is one thing. Building a framework for how to build your team, organization, department, personal brand, etc. carries with you over your lifetime. The application of that framework is what is going to be different in each environment, but you know the structure.

Simply executing the same processes from one company to the next or one job to the next, even within your same company, isn't going to be nearly as valuable as coming up with a framework to tell the story of your work, to tell the story of the impact of your work, and to tell the story of you.

Most people only stop to reflect on their accomplishments and think at this level when they leave a job and they need to update their resume. This is absolutely the wrong time to do this. What this usually means is that they were in the weeds the rest of the time.

By spending time to come up with a framework, you can bypass all the minutiae and get to a place where you can communicate your impact, plans, and your value in a coherent and confident way.

DAY 21

How to Create Unstoppable Presentations

One incredible tool in the leadership toolbox is your ability to build and deliver unstoppable presentations.

Do you know why most presentations fail?

The reason is that they're simply a regurgitation of facts or ideas and they are told from the perspective of the presenter. In these cases, the audience isn't taken into consideration and the presentation serves to inflate the ego of the presenter rather than inspire an audience or build someone else up.

The second reason is that there is no story.

There is usually a chronological series of events that either did happen or will happen. The result: the audience falls asleep. Imagine what movies would look like if they followed professional presentation templates with no real contrast, no real challenges, no heroes, no guides, just a series of events that unfold.

They'd be boring. Nobody would watch a movie.

What does storytelling have to do with presentations?

You're not telling a story in a professional context, or are you?

Story has everything to do with building an unstoppable presentation. People crave stories and talk incessantly about great ones.

There's one conference that I've presented at multiple years in a row. Since they started tracking the presenter ratings, I've always been in the top five, and in 2017, I even ranked number-one presenter at that conference.

Every year, this conference has well over two hundred presenters. These are very qualified people with big roles and titles. I beat out over two hundred people to be in that top-five category and even more to be in that number-one spot.

When I was number one, I even beat the opening keynote of the CEO who was hosting the event. He was well-known for having incredibly compelling and meaningful presentations. Let's face it, he also had the best time slot.

This achievement was something that I spent a lot of time on. I knew that if I was going to have the opportunity to be in front of an audience of more than three thousand people, or even five hundred people, or even ten people inside my organization, I was going to have to do it with story and do it in a way that would create an incredible experience in which I could bring people along with me.

And that's what I did to consistently stay in the top-five presenters every year. I spent time to figure out how to tell a story and bring my audience into that story.

Most conference presentations follow the "Here's what I did" structure.

The presenters in these cases are screaming, "Look at me. Acknowledge me for what I did. I'll tell you every step I took, every email I wrote, everything I communicated. You can learn from me and you can do this."

Whether you're working on a conference presentation or a presentation for your leadership team, you have to do a couple of key things. I've boiled all my experience down into the Five Unstoppable Presentation Must-Haves.

Unstoppable Presentation Must-Have #1— Involve your audience

This is where you break from the typical presenter role in a presentation and you engage your audience. I don't just mean asking questions such as, "How many of you have been in a leadership position before..." I want you to engage them in actual exercises, visualizations, stories, etc. You need to bring them into the story completely and get them to feel something different than just the uncomfortable seat they are sitting in. You're also going to get them to think on their feet because what you're going to present is different than anything they will have seen before.

When you cause somebody to think differently or when they're caught off guard, they're going to stay engaged. The year that I was the number-one presenter at this conference, the first five minutes were consumed with a visualization exercise. I had three thousand people in the audience, and I spent five minutes of my precious time asking them to close their eyes and envision a particular scenario that I painted.

I knew exactly what I was painting, and I knew exactly how it would make them feel. I asked them a series of questions afterward and got them to vocally respond. I told them that I didn't want them to raise their hand, I wanted to hear them. I had them shout out "Yes" if this was accurate.

For five minutes, I took them to one place, took them to another place, asked them questions. I had three thousand people completely engaged. My total presentation time was forty-five minutes but for five minutes I did nothing but take them through an experience which I scripted.

In another presentation that I did with one of my clients, I had a team of twenty-two executives inside of a large Fortune 500 company. The premise of this half-day workshop was around coming up with strategies to achieve what seemed like an unattainable goal. My job was to facilitate the entire session, and I knew I had to start it off with something very powerful.

I had all twenty-two stand up and close their eyes.

I asked them to "think about a time when you didn't know how you were going to accomplish something you had to. Think about a challenge that you faced at any point in your life. It could be from your childhood, college, post-college, professional career, etc. Think about that and keep your eyes closed."

When people close their eyes and you give them direct instructions on what to visualize, it unleashes a completely different experience.

As I went around the room, what I did was walk behind everybody. All their eyes were closed and I said, "If I tap on your shoulder, I want you to share your experience in a short summary."

I tapped on one person's shoulder, and they said, "After college, I moved to Europe with no job and no money."

That was a big challenge, and they were able to survive.

I tapped on another person's shoulder. They said, "Early on in high school I struggled with school and struggled with reading." They were able to survive.

Each time I asked someone to share, I tapped into something that they had inside of them but was deeply connected to what I was trying to teach them, which was "You got this. You've tackled seeming unattainable things before." I taught them by getting them to remember what it was like at that point in time when they had a vision for moving to Europe or accomplishing something that seemed out of reach.

I took them through this experience, and we had exceptional results. This approach was far more powerful than me getting up and saying, "When faced with a challenge, you should think about XYZ." I actually got them to experience what I was teaching them.

Unstoppable Presentation Must-Have #2—Take the audience through a story

In any presentation, you are going to have a beginning, middle, and an end. Sometimes it's helpful to start with the end.

In the conference presentation I shared, I began with the end. I took them through that experience in the first five minutes, but when I set the premise right before that, I said, "If you've ever struggled with this topic. I'm going to take you to a completely different place in forty-five minutes."

That set the stage for, "Huh, he said what? No way. He can't do that in forty-five minutes." It was the same thing with the exercise with my client. I told them that by the end of the day, "We will be united in accomplishing this seemingly unattainable goal." Then I took them through the story: beginning, middle, and end.

Unstoppable Presentation Must-Have #3— Positive and negative contrast

In the conference presentation, I used the power of contrasting positive and negative points: pain and success.

I described the pain (and I got them to experience it through visualization). Then I described what would be possible (and I got them to experience this through visualization). I described the pain again, and then I'd say what's possible.

In every instance, it was an emotional rollercoaster. First, I took them back to a previous point in time. Then, I took them to this ideal place where everything they want is completely delivered. Then, I took them back to the challenges and pains they were facing right now. Then, I took them through a little bit of success. I did this throughout the presentation.

The constant oscillation between pain and success is the contrast necessary to keep your audience engaged because they don't know what's next. If I stayed at one level and just talked about pain for forty-five minutes, I would lose everybody. Instead, I used the contrast of pain and success, happy and sad, accomplishment and disappointment, success and failure. That contrast is what creates interest. If there's no contrast, there's no interest.

In great movies, there's always a hero as well as a villain. The villain is the ultimate contrast to the hero. They stand for the opposite of what the hero does. Some people are going to identify with one side, and some are going to identify with the other side, but it's the contrast that makes it interesting. Think about the challenges between Superman and Lex Luthor or Batman and Joker.

Contrast brings excitement, interest, and energy into the story.

Unstoppable Presentation Must-Have #4— Include a surprise

This is something the audience doesn't expect. I told the audience of three thousand people that the reason they've never been able to manage their time before—which was the topic—was because their psychology sucked.

I told three thousand people that their psychology sucked. It was a shock; there was a definite gasp in the room, but it got them to pay attention. It got them to question whether their psychology was actually sound.

Another year in a different presentation on a similar topic, I told the audience that the reason they couldn't master their time was that it feels good to be needed and that they were actually fulfilling one of their human needs and feeling pleasure for themselves by being needed. I also told them that this wasn't the most productive or efficient thing they could be doing. I told them that they were selfish. Saying that the reason you can't master your time is that you're selfish is controversial, but again, it was a hook that engaged the audience midway through the presentation.

Unstoppable Presentation Must-Have #5—Bring the passion

Whatever you're talking about, it has to be the most exciting thing you could be talking about at that time. If it's not, everybody in the audience will know. If it is, they will feel your passion. When you take them on this journey, they will pay attention.

At the time of each of the presentations I shared above, I worked myself into such a frenzy over the topic that I couldn't help but explode with energy when it was time to present. I was oozing enthusiasm because I knew I could transform someone's life through my presentation.

Here are some of my trusted strategies for preparing myself to bring the passion:

1. Visualize the transformation the audience is going to have.
2. Create a mantra about why I'm going to share this information and what it's going to do for my audience.
3. Jump up and down—physical movement changes everything.
4. Close my eyes and trust that the most important thing for me to do in the world right now is to deliver for this audience.

As a leader, building this leadership skill is one of the fastest ways to be able to get your message out to more people and have a greater impact.

Download your FREE Quick-Reference Cards to take The Five Unstoppable Presentation Must-Have's with you to use in your next presentation. 30dayleadership.com/quick-reference-cards

DAY 22

Marketing and Leadership

When I became a VP, I went through a difficult period. Over a long period of time, I had been very close with the company as an advisor. I was also a coach to the CEO and several members of the executive team. I had sat in on team meetings and worked closely with the customer success team, which was my area of focus.

The company asked me numerous times over several years if I would join as VP of the department, and I declined each time because I was enjoying my consulting work.

That is until things came to a head one day. The company was in a state of transition. They were growing very fast and having some troubles with the execution of the customer success function. As an outsider and an advisor, there was only so much that I could do. I knew that if I did not step in now, bad things would happen. People were going to leave the company because of frustrations hitting an all-time high. They made me a compelling offer, I stopped consulting, and I decided to join the team.

I was very confident in my skills, I had my framework, knew what to do with the team and the customers to get everybody moving in the same direction. However, after a few short months, I found it difficult to tell the story of what I was doing. The biggest reason for that was that we couldn't see immediate results. When you can't see immediate results, regardless of who you are or what position you're in, it is very difficult to keep doubt from creeping into someone else's mind.

A couple of months after I joined, it didn't feel like anything had changed to the other executives. I would regularly tell them that we'd changed all kinds of things, however, from their point of view, nothing really changed. The same problems were occurring from a financial standpoint where customers were canceling and not renewing their contracts.

This put me in a very difficult position because I knew I was doing the right things, but I also knew that some of what I was doing wouldn't have an impact for many months. When you work with customers on an annual contract basis, it can take six, twelve, or even eighteen months to know if you have made a significant improvement because the one metric I was measured on was Net Revenue Retention. This was a measure of how many contracts renewed and expanded each quarter. Whether or not a customer renews depends on the customer's entire experience over the life of their contract.

What I overlooked was the fact that my leadership with my department was very strong, but my leadership within the executive team started very strong, based on my reputation and prior engagement, and then slowly weakened over time.

What I missed was the fact that marketing and leadership go hand-in-hand. Marketing is really all about understanding your audience and tuning your message to them. I was sharing the same message that I shared with my team with the other executives about what I was doing and how I was doing it.

What I missed was that the other executives weren't anywhere close to the same place as my team. I misunderstood my audience. I did not do an effective job of marketing my activities to build confidence. Ultimately, what happened was that they lost trust in me over time. They just saw the one metric that they cared about; they saw that as being my fault that I couldn't turn it around in a matter of months.

I knew doubt and uncertainty had crept in when I would get the same questions about when our retention was going to change? At the time, I could not figure out how to tell them what I was doing any differently.

Upon reflection, what I realized is that I was not tuning my message to my audience the same way that an expert marketer tunes his or her message to their audience. As a result of this, I began to be left out of certain conversations and then decisions. The hardest part was that some decisions were made that directly impacted me and my team and I was not part of them. I simply found out about them later. When I confronted the CEO about this, we had a rather difficult conversation.

Ultimately, this was my fault. I let doubt creep in on the part of the other executives. I did not tune my message to my audience, and their trust in me eroded because of my inability to effectively market my leadership to them.

Your message is your story. It's a story of what it is you are doing from a leadership perspective to take you, your team, your organization, your company, to the future. Your story can't be in the weeds to the point where it is too complicated, but it also can't be so pie in the sky that the audience doesn't have any context. This is where you're going to leverage the framework that we talked about previously to set goals and objectives with the rest of the executives that you work with.

Anytime you're working on sharing what it is that you do or what your plan is, the audience is critically important. What's even more important than just who the audience is, is understanding what the audience wants. That's the true secret to marketing—understanding what the audience really wants. And then, aligning what it is you're selling, which is your story, to what they want.

Your job is to tune your story to meet the needs of your audience. That's ultimately how you're going to market your leadership.

DAY 23

Managing Up

I fired my boss. This was the email I wrote to him.

"I don't need anything right now. If I need anything, I'll be in touch.
Regards,
Nils."

This happened at the end of him violating my social contract one too many times. I hit the threshold, he crossed the line, and I was not going to take it anymore. He consistently canceled our one-on-ones at the last minute. If we were scheduled to meet at 3 PM, he or his executive assistant would send me a cancelation notice or reschedule request at 2:58 PM or 2:59 PM, sometimes even at 3 PM, when I was actually in the room waiting for him. It infuriated me. He was never present with me and I couldn't count on him so I fired him. I told him I'm on my own; I'm fine.

I didn't meet with him for two months. He was my VP, but he wasn't providing what I needed.

In any leadership position, there is an element of managing up that you need to embody in your work. I'll admit that my behavior in this situation was a little extreme. However, his behavior was not something that I was going to sit by and just take again and again.

Getting moved around and constantly disappointed like this made me feel as if I just didn't matter. You have to be willing to stand up for what you believe in regardless of who's on the receiving end. Whether it's your VP, your CEO, somebody else in a leadership position, it just doesn't matter.

I probably let it go too far and did not speak up soon enough. Learning from this experience and through working with my clients, I created the following framework.

First, acknowledge your assumptions and bias. In this example, I assumed that my VP would make time for me and stick to the schedule we had in place. That was my basic assumption—if you have a meeting with me, you show up.

I remember one meeting that actually did happen. I was sitting across the conference room table from him and we were about to start. He said, "Hang on, I just need to finish this real quick." He was typing furiously and then he closed his laptop. He glanced up at me, and it looked like he had absolutely no idea where in the world he was. He literally said, "Where are we." I sarcastically said, "Right here." Even when he attended the meeting, he still wasn't able to be present, which made it feel like this was a waste of time.

Second, use the feedback formula I shared earlier. This is where you can share… Here's what I've observed… Here's the impact… Help me understand what's going on…

I admit that I did not do a great job of this until I got to the point of being so frustrated that I had to burst out and ultimately fire him as my boss. What I could have done was say, "What I've observed is that you continuously cancel our one-on-ones. Sometimes it's at the last minute, and sometimes it's at the time we're actually going to meet. The impact that has is that it makes me feel like I'm not important and that I can't trust you. Help me understand what's going on."

That would have been more productive to do before it got to the blowup.

Third, listen and ask powerful questions to understand why they did what they did. I could have asked, "What's your expectation for our one-on-ones?" Clearly, we did not have the same expectation and therefore couldn't operate with the same level of accountability.

Fourth, make a recommendation on how to move forward. After understanding more about his position, I could have made a recommendation such as, "My recommendation is that we stop our one-on-ones for a couple of months. Let's take a break. We don't need them right now. I'll be fine on my own. How does that sound?"

This would have been a bit more diplomatic than firing him, but I was so frustrated at that point that I let my emotions get the best of me. My emotional intelligence at this time was not at the highest level.

The four steps to managing up are:

1. Acknowledge your assumptions and biases
2. Use the feedback formula I shared on Day 9
3. Listen and ask powerful questions to understand their actions
4. Make a recommendation on how to move forward

Regardless of if you're dealing with the CEO, with another VP, a director, if you're managing up and follow these four steps, it will put you in a more positive place. It will hopefully alleviate the tension and the pressure that is building as a result of the situation that's causing you to have this conversation.

DAY 24

Building Relationships with Other Leaders

When I was a director at a company, I had a great relationship with the person who was the director of Sales. He was responsible for the team that sold our solution to the customers, and I was responsible for the team that worked with the customers. He and I both started out as individual contributors at this company. Over the same amount of time, we both rose through the ranks and took over the leadership roles for our respective areas.

In this role, I still had a set of accounts that I was responsible for. These were some large and strategic accounts that I kept even though I had my management responsibilities too.

One of these accounts was a very large, well-known company that paid us $100k per year for our software. This account was coming up for renewal in a couple of months. I started the renewal conversation with the Sales leader. I told him about the situation, and we started to build a strategy for how we were going to renew and expand that customer contract.

The first step was to introduce him to the client, which I did. I brought him on the call, introduced him, set the expectation that he was going to manage all the commercial terms, and I would continue supporting my client with all of our regular activities. We were off to a good start.

The Sales leader and the client had a one-on-one conversation one day to start the renewal process, and they discussed the renewal terms.

As soon as the two of them hung up the phone, my cell phone rang and it was my client. I picked up the phone and said, "Hello," and my client just let loose for a good minute or two. I just let him talk. My client was furious with what the Sales leader had told him about the terms of the renewal. The Sales leader had put out some aggressive terms, and the client did not appreciate it. He called to yell at me because he was frustrated, and I was the trusted advisor. Thankfully, I was very comfortable in that role.

After the initial rant, I asked questions such as, "Help me understand what exactly you don't like. Help me understand what you have a problem with. Help me understand what a better solution would be. Help me understand what you want."

I played the facilitator role in between the two of them where I would have this conversation with my client, talk him down off the ledge, and then share that information with my Sales leader to inform his next round of negotiations. For close to two months, after every conversation I would get an earful about the Sales leader from my client.

My relationship with the Sales leader enabled us to not only renew that customer but we doubled the annual recurring revenue of the contract. Instead of the customer paying us $100,000 a year, they now committed to paying us $200,000 a year. This was a big accomplishment, and we were recognized by our organization, which felt great.

The only way we accomplished this was by having a very deep, trusting relationship and focusing on our respective strengths. My relationship with the Sales leader was extremely strong, and as a result, I was able to be incredibly effective.

To contrast that, inside that same organization, there was a different leader on the Product and Engineering side. I'll admit that I did not have a very strong relationship with this person. When it came to advocating on behalf of our customers with Product and Engineering, I virtually was unable to get anything done!

Here I am representing the customer, sharing all the things that we need that customers want, and the Product and Engineering leader frankly didn't care. As a leader inside this organization, I missed an opportunity to build as deep a relationship with the Product and Engineering leader as I had with the Sales leader.

Had I built an equally strong relationship with the Product and Engineering leader, my outcome in getting the things that I wanted for my customers may have been different.

In any leadership position, your relationships with other leaders inside your organization are critically important. It is wise to spend as much time, effort, and energy on building those relationships internally as possible. Even if there's a tremendous amount of conflict or personality differences between you and another leader, there has to be a way to build a relationship so that ultimately you can effectively work together.

Your ability to work effectively with anyone and everyone is what's going to determine how successful you are. You cannot be successful in a leadership role if you do not have incredible relationships with other leaders inside of your organization.

DAY 25

Difficult Conversations

I had a coaching conversation with one of my clients that went something like this.

John, my coaching client, brought to the session that he was having trouble with one of his employees. When I asked him to describe it, he said the employee was one of the lowest-performing members of his team. He was uncertain about whether or not this employee would continue to be an appropriate fit at this organization or if he needed to start working on an exit plan and get HR involved.

Talking about an exit plan or an employee potentially leaving is a serious matter. I worked with him to go through the steps I'm going to show you here.

I asked, "Tell me more about this employee. Where are they underperforming?"

He said, "This employee doesn't seem to ever be on top of everything that needs to get done for his customers. He always tells me he is 'busy,' but whenever I ask questions about a customer that is deeper than surface level, he can't tell me. When he does tell me about his customers and the work he's doing, it's very tactical things. There is absolutely nothing strategic about what he's doing with his customers. I fear that if we keep him in this position, he's going to have trouble renewing customers and we're going to have trouble picking up the pieces if he were to move on."

I then asked, "What feedback have you given to this employee so far about his performance?"

My client said, "I've given him the feedback. We've had the conversations. Each time he says, 'Yep, I understand. Thanks for bringing this to my attention, I get it. I'm working on it. I'm working really hard.' Essentially, the same thing continues to happen. I feel like I have given the feedback, but I'm just not getting anywhere."

Then I asked, "Given that this is the situation with the employee, the fact that you've shared feedback with the employee, and now you're at this point where you are considering removing the employee from the organization. What would be the best next step for you?"

My client thought for a moment and said, "I think it would be having a very direct conversation with the employee, and maybe even putting them on a performance improvement plan or something. I just don't know what it's gonna take."

I replied, "In the next conversation with this employee, what would be your ideal outcome from the conversation?"

My client thought for a minute and he said, "The ideal outcome from this conversation would be that the employee understands exactly where he stands, understands where his performance is compared to the rest of the team, and he also understands how serious of a position he's in. If he doesn't change, he's not going to be working here anymore."

I said, "What I heard you say was that you have three things to accomplish in your next conversation. First of all, the employee understands exactly where he stands. Secondly, the employee understands where his performance is compared with the rest of the team. And thirdly, the employee understands how serious the position is he's in, and that if he doesn't change, he's not going to be working here anymore."

After we got this ideal outcome clear, I wanted to explore other things going on in this situation. I wanted to get my client out of the frame of mind of just focusing on this one underperforming employee who has caused a lot of stress and tension.

I asked, "What else could possibly be going on with this individual?"

My client thought for a moment and he honestly didn't know.

He said, "I don't know. I don't know why he's not performing. I don't know why it seems like he's always busy, but he's never really that productive. I don't know what else could be going on."

I said, "Let's consider that a key part of the conversation, one of your goals could be to figure out what else could possibly be going on that's contributing to this behavior."

My client agreed.

I continued, "What do you need to communicate with this employee in the most succinct and clear way?"

My client replied, "I need to tell the employee that, first of all, their performance is very low compared to the rest of the team. Secondly, their knowledge of their clients is not at the level that I expect for somebody in this role. And thirdly, that I'm concerned that they don't have what it takes to be successful here."

I said, "Great, let's pretend that I am your underperforming employee. I want you to tell me those three things exactly as if you were telling them to the underperforming employee in the meeting."

He said, "John [the employee's name], your performance as compared to the rest of the team is very low. I'm concerned about your ability to do your job effectively. If we aren't able to make some changes and improvements, there's going to be cause for looking at whether or not you're going to be successful in this role at this company."

I asked, "How do you feel about this situation now?"

My client took a deep breath and said, "I feel good. I know exactly what I need to do and exactly how to do it."

The four steps to handling difficult conversations

1. Outline the ideal outcome from the conversation
2. Try to understand what else could be going on in this person's life, either personal or professional
3. Define what you need to communicate bullet-by-bullet
4. Rehearse what you are going to say with a partner

If you're able to follow these four steps, difficult conversations will become a lot easier.

Download your FREE Quick-Reference Cards to take The Four Steps to Handling Difficult Conversations with you. 30dayleadership.com/quick-reference-cards

DAY 26

Who Knows What You Do?

I was hired by a client to do an assessment of an organization as a result of the previous VP leaving and that person's second in command taking over. Before getting started, I had a number of conversations with the organization about what was going on and ultimately, what the boundaries of the project were that I needed to execute.

I have done a lot of assessments. One of the most common requests is people want to know where their organization stands in relation to other organizations in their field / industry.

The project started and I had conversations with members of the team and the current leader. I began to unravel what was going on and how this leader was working with not only his team but also with other members of the organization.

After interviewing eight to ten people, some consistent themes started to emerge. The most troubling theme was that nobody had any idea what this leader was doing.

It had been about two months since the previous VP left, and this leader was put in charge. Over that two-month period, questions arose but were never answered. Questions such as, What was the leader doing? What was the team working on? How were they going to move forward? What are the team's major initiatives? etc.

The interesting thing was that this leader and the VP they now reported to did have regular weekly communication through a one-on-one meeting. However, both of them essentially said, "I don't know what the other one is doing."

If I boil it down to the root cause of the tension and frustration in this situation, it was simply the fact that nobody knew what this leader was doing. Ultimately, it was the responsibility of this leader to tell the story of what they were doing but that wasn't happening.

When there's an absence of clarity about you or your work, then doubts, fear, and uncertainty will creep in. That's exactly what happened with my client. The leadership of the company began to doubt whether this individual was in the right position and if they could be successful. They had no idea what this leader was doing, which is why they engaged me.

When I talked to the leader, they knew exactly what they were doing. They had a good plan in place, and they were executing against it with their team. However, nobody else knew anything about this plan outside of the team. That was the crux of the problem.

If nobody knows what you do, they will come up with answers on their own, and I guarantee that you won't like those answers.

Who knows what you do in a leadership position is an incredibly important issue. You can use all the different tools that we've covered in this book to be able to support your communication so that other people know what you do. Never allow doubt, fear, or uncertainty the chance to come into the minds of others. Always be out in front and make sure other people, especially other leaders, know what you do.

DAY 27

W3M — A Communication Framework

I had a boss who absolutely loved to write novels of feedback. It was almost like it was a personal joy for her to sit down and crank out pages and pages of email giving feedback on a call. What essentially this amounted to were her opinions about how I should be doing things differently.

It felt as if I was inadequate in every single piece of my job that I did. It was really hard to receive this kind of feedback because it was all asynchronous. It was an email with text, there was no emotion, there was no context, and there was no voice.

All it said was, you did some good things and here's a laundry list of things to improve. After a while, I eventually started ignoring these emails because I couldn't comprehend all of it. I also didn't want to spend the time to read it twelve times to absorb everything. The reality was this was how my boss chose to communicate.

Later, I realized that email was her preferred communication style. This was in direct conflict with my preferred communication style, especially in a situation where feedback was involved, which was verbal.

She missed the cue that I preferred verbal feedback over written feedback. She also spent a lot of time on these emails, but they had a very low level of impact.

As a result of this experience and many more, I created the W3M communication framework.

W3M stands for:

W -> Why?

M -> Message

M -> Medium

M -> Movement

I know you're busy. Do you know the number one thing that gets ignored when you get busy?

It's preparation.

Sitting down to think methodically about how you're going to do whatever it is you need to get done is a real challenge. The tendency is just to go straight into it and to keep moving because you have so much to do.

This is why meetings don't have agendas. This is why emails are sometimes not understood or comprehended.

The W3M framework is a simple tool to use to ensure your message gets heard.

The first step is to define your "Why"—Why do you want to send this communication or have this communication? Whether it's a presentation or an email, internal or external, whatever it is, answer simply, why am I doing this?

The second step is to define your "Message"—What do you need to convey in order to fulfill your "Why?" If the "Why" is that I need to update my leadership team on the progress that I've made in my department, then your message needs to address the progress you've made in your department. Pretty straightforward.

The third step is to define the "Medium"—This is where things get interesting because we all have habits where we communicate using certain tools like Slack, instant message, email, phone, in person, etc. Selecting the right medium comes from understanding the "Why" and looking at the message. Only after you have those two, can you decide what is the appropriate medium.

The last step is to define the "Movement"—This is the action that you want the individual to take when your message is delivered. Do you want the other person to make a decision, respond to an email, share their thoughts, speak at your next meeting, etc. The "Movement" is your way to get the person you are communicating with to take the next step.

Back to the situation with my boss who loved to write novels of feedback. If she had taken the time to work through this framework as opposed to just going through what she naturally felt comfortable doing, it could have had a dramatic impact on me from a growth standpoint. I could have absorbed and responded to the feedback that I received. Also, it could have had a dramatic impact on her, too, because my relationship with her would have been a whole lot better had I been in a position where I felt she was actually trying to help me.

The W3M formula is a way to slow down and break out of your normal habits. Your normal habits will work for you, but they may not work for other people.

Pillar 4 - Leading with Metrics

DAY 28

How to Measure Anything

"Anything can be measured."

That's what my friend said to me.

At the time, I didn't completely believe him. There were a lot of things that I felt I was doing that either didn't need to be measured or couldn't be measured. I didn't understand what he was saying.

He taught me one simple principle: Get to yes or no.

He said, "Anything you do can be boiled down to an activity. Whether or not you did an activity can be answered with a simple yes or no—the activity did or did not happen. That's how you measure it."

I then asked for an example. We were focusing heavily on time management at this time, and he shared that on a weekly basis, he would keep a scorecard of his commitments to himself from a time management perspective. He had a certain number of times a day that he would check his email, a certain amount of times each week that he would allow exceptions to his calendar. These sounded like things that were habits, but the way he made them stick was by having an accountability system that forced him to answer yes or no for each activity. That was it, there was no gray area, there was only yes or no.

I thought this was quite interesting and I decided to try it out for myself. The first area I experimented with was my email. I set an activity goal: "I will check my email no more than three times a day."

Before this approach, I was vague. I would loosely say that I wouldn't have my email open all day or that I would only scan it for important client emails, etc. What this exercise did was to help me first get clear on my activity and then quantify my target so that it could be measured.

I set the target of only checking my email three times per day. At the end of every day, I had to answer one question: "Did I meet the target?" I could only answer with a yes or no. I kept track of this answer in a spreadsheet. At the end of the week, I'd review how well I did against my target.

At the end of the first week, I looked back at the previous five days, and there was either a one or a zero in the column for that day for that particular activity. A one meant that I was successful in only checking my email three times that day. A zero meant that I was not successful and checked my email more than three times that day.

What I noticed was that there were four days with zeros and one day with a one. This told me I was not doing a great job sticking to my target of checking my email three times a day. Seeing this feedback in black and white and measuring that activity was a huge asset that helped me see something I probably would have just let slide. I probably would have said, "I'm checking it about three times a day. It's definitely less than I used to do."

What this allowed me to do was be really specific and hold myself accountable to just answering one question at the end of every day with either a yes or no. Either I did or did not meet the target.

The next week I went back and I held myself accountable to a higher level and as a result, I had three ones and two zeros. I was making progress, and by the fourth week, I was getting five ones!

Quantifying a target first and making that target answerable by a yes or no answer helped me to change my habits.

I went on to use this system and teach this system to my clients across many, many different domains and disciplines.

For example, I had a weekly meeting with my team and I had to prepare for the meeting. Many times I would do it, but sometimes I didn't do it for one reason or another. I would honestly fly by the seat of my pants in those situations. I was very comfortable in that kind of an environment, and I knew what we had to cover so I felt like sometimes I didn't really need to do the prep.

I decided to set a target that every week I would spend thirty minutes preparing for the meeting twenty-four hours in advance of the meeting. The prep always happened on the same day, and at the end of the day, I had to answer yes or no, I did or did not do the preparation.

I used the same approach with a weekly executive communication. I knew I had to send an update every week to effectively market myself and my leadership. I set a target to send out a weekly executive communication every Friday. In order to send this out on Friday, I had to have time to create the communication on Thursday. I committed to spending an hour on the communication on Thursday and then sent it out on Friday. This gave me two activities to track and hold myself accountable.

As you look at the activities that your team does on a regular basis, know that you have a system now to measure any of them. You can partner with your team to define and quantify the targets, and then you can hold them accountable.

Once an accountability system like this is in place, it's really difficult to blow it off without feeling incredibly guilty or like someone is being let down. That's okay because if the targets we set are correct, then we are driving toward the right behavior.

Download your FREE Quick-Reference Cards to remind yourself of how to measure anything. 30dayleadership.com/quick-reference-cards

DAY 29

Tracking and Reporting

Back when I was in a leadership position as a Vice President, I had a series of regular meetings with my team. Every week we had a team meeting where we reviewed our quarterly targets, the goals that we had set out to achieve that quarter. For the first five minutes of the meeting we would review the progress for the quarter to date for each of those goals.

For each metric, we looked at where we were as of that day in relation to our quarterly goal along with how much time we had left in the quarter.

I reinforced the goals, over and over again. One of the things that was really important from that leadership experience was the reminder to always reinforce the goals and never assume that someone else is thinking about the goals as much as you are.

The individual contributors on my team had a million things to think about, a million problems to solve, and a million other things to do on a daily basis. A big part of my job as the leader of that organization was to remind them continuously of the bigger picture goals that we had for the quarter and our progress toward those goals.

Whatever you're tracking and reporting, you must repeat those goals to the point where you feel like a broken record. When you feel this way, you're just getting started, keep going.

When I was looking at what metrics to report, I struggled a little bit at first with the balance between having too much and having too little. In the beginning, I had ten different metrics. Each of these ten contributed to a couple of higher-level metrics. Over time, I found that it was far more valuable to focus on the higher-level metrics than it was to try to boil the ocean and reinforce all ten. When I shared all ten metrics, everybody got confused, lost interest, or tuned out. I kept it to three key metrics for the team and reinforced those every single week.

Knowing what to track and report came down to having clarity on how the team and I were going to be measured.

What I took away from the exercise of figuring out the right balance was that not everybody had the same context. The executives had one set of context, my team members had a different set of context, and I had a completely different one, too. There was no one perfect answer right away. Over time, I figured out what was most important to report.

I asked the other executives what they wanted to know about my team and organization. I asked my team what they wanted to know about how we were performing. They wanted to know just as bad as I did, how they were doing. They wanted to know things such as, are we on track? Are we going to hit our bonus? Are we in the right place? Are we focused on the right things?

There's a small number of metrics and KPIs (I prefer three) that you can identify, track, and then reinforce in your weekly meetings and your regular communication with other executives. This can help reinforce your leadership position because everybody is going to look to you to accomplish those things which you tell them you're going to do.

What are the top three things that you need to track, report, and reinforce with your team as well as with others in the company as a representation of your team?

DAY 30

Setting Targets and Driving Accountability

One of my early bosses loved to set aggressive, completely unrealistic targets for me and the other people who worked for him. When I asked what the thinking behind this was, he said, "I always want people to stretch. I always want to motivate people to do more than they think they can. I always want to push people out of their comfort zone."

I worked under him for close to two years. During that time, I never met a single one of those goals that he set. In the beginning, I was excited because it was a new, really big challenge. Over time, what happened quarter after quarter is I never got even close to the target. It was so far beyond what was possible. As a result of this, I began to get demotivated. It motivated me less to have a very aggressive target because I never got to experience the "win" of actually meeting the target.

Anytime you've set a target in a quarter or a month or a year and you hit that target, it feels so good that you want to come back for more. You want to set another aggressive target, but you want to be able to hit it because you want that feeling again. My boss's goal was to motivate people. His approach did motivate me for a while but then it backfired. If you're setting targets that are always out of the ballpark and trying to hold people to a standard that can't be met, you run the risk of demotivation, just like I went through.

I eventually left that boss, and I really don't have that great of an opinion of my time working for him because he was so fixated on these giant potential future things that never happened. He thought he was doing everybody a favor but in reality, he was destroying motivation.

147

In the teams that I've run and the teams my coaching clients have run, when it comes to setting targets, there's a band of possibility you need to operate within. Some targets are easily achievable, some targets that may be achievable, and then there are the stretch-goal targets.

As a leader, it's really important to strike a balance that's appropriate for your team and where they are. Does your team need a boost because they've missed their targets in the last few quarters? If so, giving them a big giant hairy audacious goal that is completely unattainable probably isn't going to motivate them very much.

On the other hand, if you've gone through a series of quarters where you've missed the targets and now you give your team a very achievable, attainable, realistic goal, then you're probably going to see a different team at the end of that period when they hit the target.

Depending on where your team is, their past performance, future potential, and where you are is going to determine where to set that target. Setting the target too far can lead to demotivation. Setting the target too close can also lead to demotivation. You need to strike a balance based on the reality of your current situation.

Once you have set the targets, then it's all about accountability.

Next Steps

Where Do You Go From Here?

Before I made the shift to be the CEO of my career (the story from Day 1), I always thought that I was working for a promotion or a raise, and those were my measures of success. Each time I was rewarded or recognized for my contribution, it felt good. I realized later that this was the exact wrong approach to take. I set a standard where I felt good only when I was recognized by others. In other words, I was not in control.

After becoming the CEO of my career and taking control of every decision, I realized that personal and professional growth was far more important than a promotion or a raise. If I was in control of my personal and professional growth, I could control how I felt, and I did not need to wait for someone else to make me feel good.

This was liberating. I now had everything I needed to control my career, how I felt, and best of all, I was clear about what was important to me.

It was these choices that led me down the path to becoming a leadership coach and ultimately writing this book. In my view, you are my hero. You are on the front lines working with your team day in and day out to accomplish incredible things.

You are my hero and I am your guide. I am going to do everything possible to ensure that you are successful in becoming the leader you have always wanted to be.

I've heard people talk about how they want to work to the point where they don't have to work anymore and then volunteer their time in their community or with an organization so that they can really make an impact in other people's lives.

While this is a noble cause, what is often missing is the understanding that as a leader you have the ability to impact the lives of others every single day. You can impact the lives of those around you in a positive or negative way; it's up to you.

Great leaders are able to transition from being the hero to being the guide. Just as I am the guide for you, you are now the guide for your employees.

A world with more leaders who understand that they are the guide

151

and not the hero is a world I want to be part of.

As Catherine said at the end of the foreword, your company is very lucky to have you.

I'll add that your team is very lucky to have you, and I am very lucky to have had a chance to spend time with you. You've heard some of my most intimate stories and even some things I have never shared publicly before.

I appreciate the time and attention you are putting toward growing into the leader you have always wanted to be.

The fact that you are reading this sentence at the very end of this book shows me that you are committed to change.

I described the experience I went through with this final exercise on Day 1, and it changed the course of my life. Here's what to do…

Take a roll of masking tape and mark a line in the middle of the room. Make sure there's enough space on either side of the line to physically jump over it.

Next, think about what you are going to commit to doing now that you have been through this playbook.

When you are ready, stand to one side a few feet away from the line. Run and jump over the line, and while you are in the air, shout as loud as you can what you commit to doing.

What I yelled out as I flew over that line in 2012 was "I commit to sharing my gift of coaching with the world."

I'm thankful you have given me the opportunity to share my gift and be your guide.

With Gratitude,
Nils Vinje
Founder and CEO of 30 Day Leadership
30dayleadership.com

Work with Me

You now know more about leadership than most people ever will. However, knowing about leadership is not enough. You must put these strategies into action. As you put everything into action, you're going to have questions and need additional coaching. I'll always be here as your guide. There are a number of ways I can continue to support you in becoming the leader you have always wanted to be. Visit 30dayleadership.com/products to explore the coaching options and find the right fit for you.

Leave a Review on Amazon

I'd greatly appreciate it if you would you leave a review of 30 Day Leadership Playbook on Amazon. Here are a few prompts to get you started, all you need to do is fill in the blank.

Before I read this book, I thought leadership was…

After reading 30 Day Leadership Playbook, I feel…

The number one thing I took away from this playbook is…

I put [insert lesson] into action and saw [result] within [timeframe]…

This playbook will teach you…

I'm glad I read 30 Day Leadership Playbook because…

The biggest impact this book had on me is…

You should read this book if you…

Get Your FREE Gift!

My mission is to empower you to become the leader you have always wanted to be.

To get the best experience with this book, I've found that readers who download and use the

30 Day Leadership Playbook Quick-Reference Cards

are able to implement faster and take the steps needed to become the leader they have always wanted to be.

Download the Quick-Reference Cards for FREE today by visiting:

30dayleadership.com/quick-reference-cards

About The Author

Nils Vinje is the founder and CEO of 30DayLeadership.com. He is a leadership coach, consultant, speaker, and author. Nils inspires people everywhere to become the leader they have always wanted to be. Nils lives in Phoenix, Arizona with his wife, three kids and two dogs.

Made in the USA
Monee, IL
03 December 2020

TESTIMONIES FOR THE CHURCH

VOLUME ONE